# Raising Poultry

*The Ultimate Backyard Companion, Covering Chickens, Turkeys, Geese, Ducks, Guineas, Game Birds, and a Variety of Fowl*

# Table of Contents

# Introduction

Raising poultry is one of the most fulfilling endeavors you can embark on. This first step – reading this book – will unlock a new world of understanding the complex life of the birds you choose to farm. It provides a wide range of valuable tips, methods, and techniques for poultry farming that are hands-on, practical, easy to read, and suitable for beginners. These are delivered with an entertaining flavor that keeps you engaged until the end.

You will learn the details of housing poultry and keeping their health and wellness up to par. You will also learn the tools necessary for breeding your birds and understanding their psychology and social dynamics. Furthermore, you will learn to ethically farm sustainably and environmentally friendly. From top to bottom, everything you need to know about raising the birds of your choice is outlined with nutritional details and habitat requirements.

Since raising animals, especially birds, without the proper knowledge could have disastrous outcomes, you have made the right choice by picking up this book. It unpacks poultry farming in detail; carefully reading each section places you in a position to excel. As you work through the chapters, your eyes will be opened to the most commonly overlooked factors and considerations. By shining a light on the complexities of raising poultry, you will be put in an amazing position to succeed as a beginner. Many people desire to farm but never start because they have no idea how to get the ball rolling. The start-to-finish outline of the intricacies of poultry farming provided in these pages will make building your coop easier than you ever thought possible.

As you get into it, you will gain the skills that can only be learned through experience. Poultry farming provides meat, eggs, or companions if you want some feathered friends. A little bit of elbow grease and commitment can help you set up an operation that runs smoothly for years to come. Don't be scared. Take that risk and jump right into the deep end. You will not regret becoming a poultry farmer!

# Chapter 1: Backyard Poultry 101

Do you know that birds are the descendants of dinosaurs? Yes, those cute and small creatures evolved from huge and scary reptiles. How is it possible that all dinosaurs have been extinct for millions of years? This can't be another case of Jurassic Park, right? Well, not exactly. One lineage survived that catastrophic comet. That was the birds. Although all birds come from the dinosaur family tree, chickens are more primitive than all others. They also resemble dinosaurs the most. Basically, when you are raising chickens, you have tiny dinosaurs running around in your backyard.

Raising poultry has many benefits; it isn't just having a constant supply of fresh products. This chapter covers these benefits, the common misconceptions about poultry, and some of the birds you can raise.

## Why Backyard Poultry?

If you are hesitant about having backyard birds, this section will change your mind. There is a reason these funny and feathery creatures are very popular among both farmers and non-farmers. Wouldn't you love to have access to fresh eggs all the time? Besides the obvious benefits, raising poultry is also an extremely rewarding experience.

There is a reason these funny and feathery creatures are very popular among both farmers and non-farmers.

Whether you want to start a small business, keep these birds as pets, or simply live a self-sufficient and greener lifestyle, there are so many benefits to reap from backyard poultry.

## Fresh Products

The most apparent advantage of raising poultry is getting fresh eggs. These are much healthier and environmentally friendly than the ones you buy at the grocery store. They don't go through shipping or processing, which can put them at risk. You will also be involved in every step, from choosing the birds to collecting and storing the eggs. You are in control of what to feed your birds and which environmental conditions are best to guarantee safe produce that will give you peace of mind. You won't have to worry about pesticides, steroids, chemicals, hormones, or unethical farming practices.

Fresh eggs also taste better and are richer in color. Unlike store-bought ones, they don't contain as much bad cholesterol or saturated fats.

Have you noticed the prices of organic eggs in the supermarket lately? Raising farm birds will save you a lot of money in the long run. If you plan to sell them, you will also make a good profit.

You can raise birds for their meat instead of buying it from unethical farms. You will have access to a natural meat resource free of hormones.

This creates a synergy between you and your birds as they depend on you for survival, and you depend on them for sustenance.

## Environmentally Friendly

As you won't rely on commercial egg production, you can positively impact the environment by raising your own poultry. Big farms usually rely on water, lighting, and electricity, which harm the planet. Raising farm birds, on the other hand, requires fewer resources. It reduces your carbon footprint and allows you to do your part to protect the environment.

Backyard poultry also provides you with a more sustainable option, making you directly involved in your food supply chain. You will become self-reliant and less dependent on commercial goods. This lifestyle will make you more appreciative of all the natural resources contributing to your meals.

## Low Maintenance

When people decide to become self-sufficient and raise farm animals, they usually prefer to raise birds over cows or sheep. Unlike most animals, birds easily adapt and are self-sufficient. They are extremely low maintenance and don't require much responsibility. All you need to do is set up a living space for them. Things get much easier afterward since they can take care of themselves.

Raising chickens, ducks, etc., will be a great first step if you plan on expanding and venturing into livestock or farming.

## Great Company

Birds can bring joy to your life. These cute and funny little creatures can liven up your backyard for hours on end. They are very interesting birds. They love exploring the world around them and play just like children. You can have breakfast every morning in your backyard and watch them peck around for seeds or establish their pecking order. This can be very therapeutic and help you connect with nature and unwind. Kids will also enjoy playing and running around with them.

Birds are amusing creatures with gentle sounds that can reduce anxiety and calm you. After a long day at work, spending time with your birds will give you peace of mind and make you forget about all the stress you experienced during the day.

## Producing Fertilizers

Chickens and other birds produce manure rich in nutrients, which acts as a natural fertilizer. It contains potassium, phosphorus, and nitrogen that encourage plant growth. Manure can improve the soil's fertility and nutrient content so plants can thrive. This results in an eco-friendly garden. Using manure to fertilize your soil is a sustainable way to feed your plants and reduce your dependence on unnatural alternatives.

## Gardening

Having backyard poultry in your garden can boost its health, output, and even its fertility. Chickens reduce pests since they feed on various organisms like snails and grasshoppers, which can damage your garden. They also eat ticks and mosquitoes, so you and your family can spend time outdoors during the spring and summer without worrying about insect bites.

Chicken can also reduce weed growth by scratching and pecking to dig up seeds. They can loosen the soil, which encourages plant growth.

## Making a Small Business

If you want to earn extra cash, you can sell the meat or eggs to friends, family, local restaurants, or farmer's markets.

## Kids Will Love Them

You can raise poultry for their eggs and meat, but your child may want to keep one as a pet. This will teach them responsibility and to love and care for something other than themselves. They will also want to spend more time outdoors to play with their bird pet and get some fresh air instead of staying at home and playing video games.

## Eating Kitchen Scraps

Backyard chickens eat kitchen scraps, which reduces the trash output. They can eat anything, even meat. Yes, that's right. Chickens are carnivores, and many people feed them on meat or even other bird bones. Collect all the scraps daily in a big bowl with your leftover food and leave it in your chicken coop. They will enjoy it.

## More Humane

Have you ever seen how industrial farms treat birds and animals? They are kept in small spaces just for breeding. They can't leave their quarters to walk around, play, stretch their wings, or socialize with other birds. By raising your own poultry, you won't be supporting these farms.

According to a 2010 Cambridge University study, birds that can move around freely and peck for food produce more nutritious eggs with higher omega-3 fatty acids and vitamin E levels than eggs from industrial farms.

### Therapy Animals

You often see people adopting a cat or a dog to help them cope with their anxiety, ADHD, or other mental health problems. Did you know that birds can be therapeutic as well? Many countries use them as therapy animals in nursing homes where residents care for them and sell their eggs.

### Improve Your Mental Health

Keeping birds as pets can reduce stress, increase resilience, fulfill your social needs, boost self-esteem, and teach responsibility, especially to kids. It can also improve social relationships, reduce loneliness and depression, and improve overall well-being.

### Improves Physical Health

You will notice an improvement in your physical health since you eat organic meat and food with higher nutrients. Organic eggs contain less cholesterol, more beta carotene, and fatty acids than store-bought eggs.

### Pest Control

Did you know that one chicken can clear bugs from 120 square feet of land every week? Chickens aren't picky eaters and can feed on grubs, beetles, and all types of insects. Basically, they will eat any insect that crosses their path.

### Bird Watching

Bird-watching is extremely therapeutic. Getting out in the fresh air will make you feel rejuvenated. It also allows you to spend time alone in nature without any distractions so you can unwind and calm your nerves. It also keeps the mind active and improves memory, especially in dementia patients.

### Sense of Accomplishment

Raising your own poultry will give you a sense of accomplishment and drive you to chase your dreams and goals. You believe, "If I can take care of these beautiful creatures, I can do anything."

# Common Myths Debunked

You have probably heard a few things about poultry keeping that have discouraged you from raising chickens or other birds at home. There is a lot of misinformation about the subject that will be cleared up in this section.

### Myth #1: Raising Poultry for Meat Is Expensive

This isn't true. Although feeding costs are on the rise, it is still cheaper to raise poultry at home. In fact, one pound of organic backyard poultry costs less than one pound of store-bought meat.

### Myth #2: Bird Meat Is Harmful

If you choose the right birds, feed them properly, and care for their well-being, you won't face any problems, and your birds' meat will be healthy and delicious.

### Myth #3: Raising Birds for Meat Is Time-Consuming

Whether you are raising poultry for meat or eggs, birds are low-maintenance and self-sufficient. Caring for them is easy and will only take 10 to 20 minutes daily.

### Myth #4: Birds Raised for Meat Are Violent

Birds raised for meat, like any other bird, love to play, sit in the shade, and won't fight back if your child picks them up or plays with them.

### Myth #5: Chickens Are Noisy

Do you remember that Friends episode when Chandler and Joey's chicken woke Rachel and Monica up? Although it turned out to be a rooster, most people think all chickens are loud and will disturb them, their families, and their neighbors. Roosters may be loud, but hens are generally quiet except when startled or laying eggs.

### Myth #6: Birds Have a Bad Odor

This is another common misconception that couldn't be further from the truth. In fact, birds are very clean and usually preen their feathers or dust bathing. So, if you notice a bad odor, it is probably because the coop needs cleaning.

### Myth #7: Hens Lay Eggs Every Day

Do you think chickens would survive if they laid eggs every day? This myth came from children's story books and illustrations that show chickens doing nothing but sitting on their nests. Most breeds produce three eggs a week.

### Myth #8: Backyard Poultry Attract Wild Animals

Some believe backyard poultry attracts rats, coyotes, raccoons, and other wild animals. However, those animals are drawn to pet bowls, wild bird feeders, garbage, barbecue grills, or backyard compost, but never to your birds.

### Myth #9: You Will Need Roosters

It is understandable why many people have this misconception. They believe that you will need a male (rooster) and a female (hen) to create babies or eggs. Although this is true, it doesn't apply to shell eggs. This is a natural process all hens go through without the help of a rooster.

### Myth #10: Blue and Brown Eggs Are Bad

Many people believe that eggs are dirty or rotten if they aren't white. That is false. The color of the eggshell changes depending on the bird's breed. There are different colors of eggshells, like pink, blue, and brown, and they are all safe to consume.

### Myth #11: Raising Poultry Lowers Property Value

Your neighbor might tell you to eliminate your birds because they are lowering the neighborhood's value. There is no evidence that raising poultry in your backyard impacts the property value.

### Myth #12: Birds' Eggs Are Difficult to Harvest

This can only be true if you use the wrong nest boxes. If you provide one box for every five hens, they will easily lay their eggs, and you won't have any difficulty harvesting them.

### Myth #13: Chicken Carry Diseases

This is an old myth that many people still believe today. Chickens are clean animals and are extremely safe to consume and handle. In fact, they can protect you from diseases by removing pests from your garden. It never hurts to wash your hands after handling your birds, though.

### Myth #14: You Can't Raise Poultry in the City

As long as you have a small yard, you can raise poultry whether you live in the country or the city.

### Myth #15: Roosters Only Crow in the Morning

Although roosters crow every day at dawn to greet the morning, they also crow during the day.

### Myth #16: Chickens Are Dumb

Chickens have always been associated with cowardice and lack of intelligence. However, they are brave and intelligent animals you can teach to recognize colors, do tricks, and count.

### Myth #17: You Can't Have Birds If You Live Near Predators

Predators are everywhere, and this shouldn't stop you from raising poultry. You can do things to protect your birds, like adding netting or installing a predator apron.

### Myth #18: You Should Only Raise the Same Type of Birds Together

You can raise different types of birds and chickens together.

### Myth #19: Bird Coops Must Be Heated

Some types of birds, like chickens, thrive in cold weather, and heaters should be avoided since they are a fire hazard.

### Myth #20: Bird Coops Are Ugly

Birds' coops come in different colors and styles, and many can be nice decor for your backyard.

# Different Types of Poultry Birds

This section focuses on different types of poultry birds so you can decide which one is right for you to raise.

There are different types of poultry birds, so you must decide which one is right for you to raise.
https://commons.wikimedia.org/wiki/File:Scheuerer_H%C3%BChnerhof.jpg

# Chickens

Chickens are the most popular backyard birds in the world. You can raise them for meat, eggs, or as pets. They usually start laying eggs between 16 and 18 weeks old.

**Most Common Breeds:**

- Sussex
- Orpington
- Leghorn
- New Hampshire
- Rhode Island

**Distinctive Characteristics:**

- Average size
- Small heads
- Short wings
- Short beaks
- Featherless legs
- Round body
- Four claws on each foot

**Needs:**

- A nest to lay eggs
- Other chickens
- Exercises
- Coops
- Coop cleaning
- Collecting eggs
- Protection from predators and the weather

**Fun Fact:** *Chickens have great memories. They can recognize about 100 distinct humans and fowls. If you are ever separated from your chicken, it will most likely remember you when it sees you.*

# Ducks

Ducks live in water and on land and can fly as well. They are commonly raised in the U.S., U.K., and the Netherlands. Like chicken, people raise them for their meat and eggs. They also sell their feathers. A female duck is called "duck," and a male duck is called "drake." They lay about 300 eggs a year.

**Most Common Breeds:**
- Domestic duck
- Whistling duck
- Teal
- Sea duck
- Perching duck

**Distinctive Characteristics:**
- Long, flat bill
- Webbed feet
- Short necks
- Small size

**Needs:**
- A healthy diet
- Protection from the weather
- Sunlight
- Water for swimming
- Protection from predators

*Fun Fact: Ducks have waterproof feathers, so they can move and fly easily when out of the water.*

# Pigeons

People raise pigeons for sport, as messengers, or for their meat. They start nesting when they are about 30 days old and lay eggs daily.

**Most Common Breeds:**
- Utility breed
- Fancy breed
- Fliers

**Distinctive Characteristics:**
- Small
- Gentle

- Plump
- Bobbing head
- Long wings

**Needs:**
- Pigeon aviary
- Other pigeons
- Protection against harsh weather and predators
- Exercises
- Wood shavings
- Clean water

*Fun Fact: If a pigeon sees a picture of itself and other birds, it can recognize itself. They can also differentiate between pictures of different people.*

# Turkey

Turkey is one of the biggest types of poultry in the world. They are mainly raised for meat production. Although they lay eggs, consuming them isn't that common. In Africa, people raise them as pets or for security. They produce 45 eggs yearly, each taking 28 days to hatch. In America, people usually eat their meat on Thanksgiving and Christmas.

**Life Stages:**
- **Roasters:** Turkeys under four months
- **Hens:** Female turkeys around five months
- **Tom:** Male turkeys at 12 months
- **Mature:** Turkeys over 15 months

**Most Common Breeds:**
- Bourbon reds
- Blue state
- Black turkey
- Beltsville small white

**Distinctive Characteristics:**
- Long red ornament
- A fleshy wattle on the throat
- Black feathers

- Dark with a bronze-green iridescence

**Needs:**
- Food
- Water
- Bedding
- Heat
- Nests
- A safe place to run

*Fun Fact: Turkeys' heads change color to reflect their mood and emotions. For instance, if they are terrified, their heads can turn red.*

# Geese

Similar to ducks, geese live in water and on land. They were raised by the ancient Egyptians thousands of years ago and were the first type of poultry to be domesticated. People raise them for meat and egg production; some sell their feathers. They produce about 65 eggs per year.

**Most Common Breeds:**
- Toulouse
- Lands
- Kuban
- Huoyan goose
- Czechoslovakian White
- Embden

**Distinctive Characteristics:**
- Short necks
- Humped bill at the base
- Legs further forward than ducks

**Needs:**
- Clean water
- Protection from predators
- Grass
- Kiddie pool for swimming

*Fun Fact: Geese mate for life, are extremely loyal to their partners, and are protective of their offspring.*

# Quail

People raise quails for egg and meat production. Their eggs are used for medicinal purposes and to treat multiple conditions like allergies. They eat berries, leaves, seeds, and insects. They lay 200 eggs annually, each taking 23 days to hatch.

**Most Common Breeds:**
- Gambel's quail
- British Range quail
- English White quail
- Italian quail
- Japanese quail

**Distinctive Characteristics:**
- Small body
- Long pointed wings
- Curved, short beaks
- Long, brown legs

**Needs:**
- Food
- Water
- Clean shelter
- Protection against harsh weather

**Fun Fact:** *Quail can camouflage and blend in with their surroundings to hide from predators.*

Raising poultry is a fun and relaxing hobby. You will feel a sense of accomplishment as you care for these birds and watch them grow. In addition to consuming safe and clean products, your mental health and well-being will thrive.

# Chapter 2: Choosing the Right Birds

The key to raising poultry is making informed decisions right from the start. You need to consider selecting the right birds, the unique characteristics of your backyard, personal objectives, and the level of care you can provide. This chapter aims to give insights into the considerations shaping your choices.

## Considerations for Poultry Selection

### Space Constraints

The available space in your backyard plays a role in the type and number of birds you can keep. Consider the size of the coop and the outdoor area for free-ranging. Certain breeds are well-suited for smaller spaces, while others thrive in bigger environments. Understanding your space constraints is crucial for the health and well-being of your birds. The Brahma chicken, for example, thrives well in smaller spaces, whereas the Delaware chicken prefers living in large coops.

### Climate Compatibility

Different poultry breeds exhibit varying levels of adaptability to climate conditions. Some breeds are built to withstand cold temperatures, while others can only survive in fairly warmer climates. Knowing the region's climate and the temperature shifts during seasonal changes provides insights to make the selection easier and ensure your poultry remains comfortable and productive throughout the seasons.

## Purpose

Ask yourself why you want to raise poultry. Are you looking for a fresh supply of eggs? Do you need to raise poultry for meat? Will this be a hobby? Or do you want to experiment before expanding? Whatever it is, having the reason in mind narrows down your options. For example, some bird species are renowned for their meat quality, while others have a striking appearance. Having a clear idea of why you want to raise birds will save you time and allow you to pick a breed that aligns with your goals.

## Amount of Care Required

Be honest about how much time and effort you can dedicate to care. Some breeds are more independent and require minimal maintenance, making them suitable for beginners or individuals with busy schedules. Other breeds may demand more attention, especially regarding grooming, health monitoring, and specialized care.

# Common Poultry Types and Considerations

## Egg-Laying Breeds

If your primary goal is a consistent supply of fresh eggs, consider breeds renowned for their laying capabilities.

*https://www.pexels.com/photo/a-chick-and-eggs-on-a-nest-6897497/*

If your primary goal is a consistent supply of fresh eggs, consider breeds renowned for their laying capabilities. Popular choices include the

Rhode Island Red, Leghorn, and Sussex. These breeds are known for their reliability in egg production and are well-suited for backyard enthusiasts looking for a daily output.

### Meat-Producing Breeds

For those interested in homegrown meat, breeds like the Cornish Cross or the Broiler are common choices. These are bred for efficient and rapid growth, providing a source of high-quality meat for your table. They may require more care and attention to ensure optimal growth and well-being.

### Dual-Purpose Breeds

Dual-purpose breeds, like the Plymouth Rock or the Australorp, are versatile choices that balance egg production and meat quality. These breeds are well-suited for backyard settings where eggs and meat are desired, providing a comprehensive sustainable poultry-keeping solution.

### Ornamental Breeds

For those seeking the aesthetic charm of poultry, ornamental breeds like the Silkie or the Polish chicken are popular choices. They often feature unique plumage, distinctive color patterns, or captivating personalities, adding a delightful touch to your backyard environment. Keep in mind that ornamental breeds may have specific care requirements.

# Considerations for Poultry Selection

Here are some considerations when selecting poultry breeds and real-life scenarios that reveal how each factor influences the selection.

### Space Constraints

- Evaluate the square footage of your backyard and assess the space available for the coop and outdoor roaming. Consider breeds suitable for confined spaces if your backyard is limited.
- Provide ample space to prevent stress and territorial disputes among your flock.
- Understand that larger, more active breeds may require more room.
- Consider the layout of your backyard, including trees, bushes, and other structures, to ensure a well-organized and safe environment.

The Johnsons, nestled in the suburbs with a petite backyard, chose Bantam chickens. Their small size and gentle nature suited the limited space and brought a delightful charm to the family, turning the backyard into a miniature haven for their feathered friends.

## Climate Compatibility

- Research your region's climate, considering temperature extremes, humidity, and other weather factors.
- Choose breeds known for their adaptability to your specific climate, ensuring they remain comfortable and healthy throughout the seasons.
- Implement appropriate shelter and ventilation measures based on your climate to safeguard your poultry.
- Plan for seasonal changes and extreme weather events, providing additional protections when needed.

Up in the northern reaches, the Thompsons faced biting winters. Opting for resilient breeds like the Plymouth Rock and Wyandotte was not just a choice but a necessity. These cold-hardy birds weathered the chill and added a sense of resilience to the Thompsons' homestead.

## Purpose

- Research breeds that align with your goals – some excel in egg production, others in meat quality, and certain breeds are prized for their ornamental characteristics.
- Align your purpose with the inherent traits of the chosen breeds to maximize productivity.
- Consider the market demand for specific poultry products in your area if your purpose includes potential sales.

Fueled by a passion for sustainability, Maria found her purpose in heritage breeds. The Sussex and Dorking, with their historical significance, became not just layers of eggs or sources of meat but ambassadors of conservation, preserving genetic diversity and connecting Maria to a broader community of like-minded enthusiasts.

## Amount of Care Required

- Assess your daily schedule and be realistic about the time and effort you can dedicate to poultry care.
- Different breeds have varying care requirements; some are more independent and low-maintenance, while others may

need meticulous grooming, health monitoring, and specialized care.

- Consider your experience and choose breeds that match your comfort level and resources.

- Research specific health considerations for each breed, including susceptibility to common diseases and required vaccinations.

The Millers, juggling the chaos of family life, gravitated toward low-maintenance breeds. The Rhode Island Red and Australorp supplied fresh eggs with minimal fuss and became resilient companions, perfectly fitting into their busy daily lives.

The goal can extend beyond eggs, meat, and ornamental purposes. Here's a scenario for inspiration. The Petersons, grappling with a persistent slug invasion, took in Khaki Campbell ducks. Beyond their role as pest controllers, these quacking allies added a playful element to the Petersons' backyard, turning an everyday task into a spectacle of nature's quirky pest management.

## Behavioral Characteristics

- Understand the temperament and behavior of different poultry breeds. Some breeds are docile and easily handled, while others may be more skittish or territorial.

- Consider the social dynamics of each breed, especially if you plan to keep multiple types of poultry. Some breeds thrive in flocks, while others exhibit aggressive behavior.

- Evaluate noise levels, especially if you have close neighbors. Some breeds are known for being quieter than others.

Choosing suitable poultry breeds demands meticulous attention to detail and considerations like space, climate, purpose, care requirements, behavioral traits, egg and meat characteristics, and the unique qualities of each breed. After thinking about these factors, optimize the conditions for your poultry and set the stage for a fulfilling and sustainable poultry-keeping experience.

## Purpose-Driven Selection

Selecting suitable poultry breeds is often purpose-driven, with specific goals shaping enthusiasts' and farmers' choices. Whether the aim is abundant egg production, high-quality meat, an ornamental display, or contributing to conservation efforts, each purpose influences bird selection in distinctive ways.

### Egg Production

For those prioritizing a consistent supply of fresh eggs, breeds renowned for their prolific laying capabilities become the top choice. Considerations include the number of eggs per week, egg size, and the ability to sustain egg production throughout the year.

- Assess the balance between egg quantity and size based on your preferences and requirements.
- Consider factors beyond egg quantity, like color and taste.
- Explore breeds known for producing specific types of eggs, like those with brown, white, or colored shells.
- Research the nutritional content of eggs produced by different breeds.
- Assess whether you prefer breeds that lay consistently or exhibit seasonal variations in egg production.
- Research egg-laying capabilities, considering the number of eggs laid weekly, egg size, and persistence throughout the year.
- Explore the potential for broodiness, as some breeds may be more inclined to hatch eggs.

**Top Choices:** Leghorns, Rhode Island Reds, and Sussex are favored for their impressive egg-laying prowess, making them ideal selections for egg-centric goals.

### Meat Production

When the primary objective is raising poultry for high-quality meat, breeds with efficient growth rates, good feed conversion, and tender meat are the go-to. The focus is on breeds that deliver optimal meat yield without compromising taste and texture.

- Understand the growth rate and feed efficiency of meat-producing breeds.
- Acknowledge the need for attentive care and controlled growth to ensure optimal health and meat quality.
- Research the processing requirements for different meat-producing breeds, including their suitability for home processing.
- Research the taste, texture, and tenderness of meat produced by different breeds.

- Consider the growth rate of meat-producing breeds and how it aligns with your timeline.
- Explore heritage breeds known for superior meat quality and flavor.
- Understand the processing requirements for meat production, including potential challenges associated with specific breeds.
- Explore breeds that offer a balance between egg production and meat quality, providing a comprehensive solution for sustainable poultry keeping.
- Consider dual-purpose breeds like the Plymouth Rock or Australorp for both egg and meat production.
- Acknowledge that these breeds may excel less than specialized breeds in either category but offer a well-rounded option.
- Research the average lifespan of dual-purpose breeds to plan for long-term sustainability.

**Top Choices:** Broilers, Cornish Cross, and heritage breeds like Dorking are popular for those aiming for superior meat production.

### Ornamental Display

Individuals looking to enhance the aesthetic appeal of their flock often prioritize breeds known for striking plumage, unique color patterns, or captivating personalities. The emphasis is on breeds that serve as living artworks, adding visual charm to the surroundings.

- Recognize the unique characteristics of ornamental breeds, such as distinctive plumage, color patterns, or captivating personalities.
- Understand that ornamental breeds, like the Silkie or Polish chicken, may have specific care requirements, including grooming and protection from predators.
- Consider the aesthetic appeal and temperament of ornamental breeds to enhance the visual charm of your backyard.
- Explore breeds with unique behavioral traits, such as breeds known for being particularly friendly or those with entertaining behaviors.

Top Choices: Silkie chickens, Polish chickens, and ornamental bantams are sought after for their distinctive and visually appealing features, contributing to an ornamental display.

## Heritage Breeds

People involved in conservation are primarily concerned with *breed conservation*. However, before starting conservation efforts, it's necessary to consider the following factors and understand the specific requirements of the breed to ensure they thrive in the provided conditions.

- Explore heritage breeds known for their historical significance, resilience, and adaptability.
- Consider the conservation aspects of raising heritage breeds to contribute to preserving genetic diversity.
- Acknowledge that heritage breeds may have slower growth rates and different egg-laying patterns than modern commercial breeds.
- Research the unique characteristics and cultural importance of specific heritage breeds.

## Conservation

Conservation-minded individuals contribute to preserving genetic diversity and rare poultry breeds facing endangerment. They focus on raising breeds at risk, helping maintain a living gene pool, and preventing the loss of valuable genetic traits.

**Top Choices**: Breeds like the Delaware, Dominique, or Cream Legbar, classified as threatened or critical, become ambassadors for genetic conservation, fostering a sense of responsibility toward poultry biodiversity.

Understanding the purpose behind poultry selection dictates the traits and characteristics prioritized in the chosen breeds. Whether aiming for prolific egg layers, superior meat quality, an ornamental ensemble, or active participation in conservation, aligning bird choices with specific goals ensures a purpose-driven and fulfilling poultry-keeping experience.

# Bird Temperament

When it comes to poultry keeping, understanding the intricacies of bird temperaments is a fundamental aspect that can significantly impact the overall well-being of the flock. This involves knowing the breed's behavioral aspects, their compatibility with other birds, and the suitability of specific breeds for families with children or other pets.

## Behavioral Aspects

Each poultry breed has unique behavioral traits that influence how they interact with their environment and caretakers. For instance, breeds like the Rhode Island Red, known for their docile temperament, are often more amenable to handling and human interaction. Conversely, with their energetic disposition, breeds like the Leghorn may thrive in more active and free-ranging setups. Recognizing and understanding these behavioral nuances allows poultry keepers to create an environment that aligns with their preferred level of interaction and the overall experience they seek in poultry keeping.

## Compatibility with Other Birds

Poultry, by nature, is social. Some breeds exhibit communal and tolerant behaviors, creating a cooperative and harmonious environment when housed together. Other breeds may display territorial tendencies or aggression, influencing the social dynamics of the flock. Breeds celebrated for their friendly and sociable nature, like Sussex or Australorp, are excellent choices for mixed flocks. This understanding keeps the social structure within the flock cohesive and stress-free.

## Suitability for Families

Introducing poultry into a family setting requires consideration of how well a particular breed adapts to interactions with children or other pets. Some breeds inherently possess gentle and patient temperaments, making them ideal companions in family environments. Silkie chickens, for example, are renowned for their gentle disposition and are often well-suited for families with children. Being mindful of a breed's tolerance levels ensures a positive and enriching experience for all household members, promoting safe and enjoyable interactions.

Some breeds inherently possess gentle and patient temperaments, making them ideal companions in family environments.

*https://www.pexels.com/photo/girl-playing-with-chicken-on-pink-studio-background-5263998/*

Likewise, getting family members on board is crucial when raising poultry in the backyard. It's beneficial for the breeds you want to raise as it increases the level of care the birds will receive, ensuring they thrive without an issue. If you have small children, educate them on these birds and demonstrate over time about adequate poultry care, how they can approach these feathered cuties, and build a bond of trust. Teaching these skills enhances the child's understanding of nature and increases their positive personality attributes like empathy, providing care, and decision-making.

Issues like overcrowding, raising different breeds in a confined space, poor nutrition, lack of attention, and numerous other factors can further deteriorate bird temperament. In the coming chapters, you will learn more about housing, care, nutrition, incubation, and much more; several of these components of poultry raising affect bird temperament. The practical tips listed below can make a difference and guarantee that your birds thrive without a problem.

- Frequently visit your feathered friends, making your presence a non-threatening part of their environment.
- You can use treats or small amounts of their favorite feed to create a positive association with human interaction.
- Take your reinforcement training to the next level by using a clicker. The breed you raise will slowly associate the clicking sound with treats or positive interactions with their caretaker.
- Avoid putting too many birds in a limited space, as it only leads to aggression and stress and increases the risk of developing diseases.
- When preparing the housing area, select a quiet and noise-free place.
- Be consistent in the feeding times and ensure the feed is nutritious and balanced.
- Whether you alone – or with the whole family – have a consistent team of caretakers so the birds can become familiar with faces that come daily to provide care.
- During inspections or maintenance, avoid catching and handling the birds aggressively.
- When clipping wings, perform it gently to avoid distressing the birds.
- Whenever you notice a bird exhibiting aggressive behavior, separate the bird immediately and keep it under monitoring to address the cause of this aggressive behavior.
- Instead of feeding them in one specific area, implement foraging opportunities by scattering grains or seeds on a larger area if possible.
- Nearby predators can also cause distress in the flock, which must be mitigated as soon as possible.
- Introduce hanging objects and interactive toys to improve their overall mood.
- Always keep the coop clean and maintain feasible temperature and humidity. Birds can develop stress in unhealthy environments and even become prone to several diseases.

A comprehensive understanding of bird temperaments involves recognizing the unique behavioral aspects of each breed and considering their compatibility within a flock and their suitability for specific family dynamics. Ensuring the flock stays healthy, thriving, and calm involves paying attention to nutrition, housing, disease prevention, brooding, and much more. Understanding the overall picture and taking informed steps is the right way forward. Maintaining this thoughtful approach guarantees that the chosen poultry breeds contribute to a harmonious, enjoyable, and enriching experience for poultry keepers and their feathery friends.

# Chapter 3: Housing, Nesting, and Rooting

Creating an optimal living space for your feathered friends is paramount to their well-being, productivity, and health. This chapter delves into the importance of a well-designed habitat, exploring its impact on various aspects of avian life. You'll find several examples to guide you in crafting suitable housing setups tailored to different backyard sizes and budgets.

## The Necessity of a Well-Designed Space

A well-designed living space for birds is not just a physical structure; it is a pivotal factor that profoundly influences your avian companions' overall well-being, productivity, and health. In this section, you'll explore in detail why a carefully planned habitat is essential for creating a haven that contributes to the holistic welfare of poultry birds.

When designing the coop, nesting and perching areas must be properly assigned.
*https://www.pexels.com/photo/wooden-hen-house-with-straw-baskets-on-shelves-4577546/*

## Promoting Well-Being

A thoughtfully designed habitat allows birds to improve their mental and physical well-being. This includes perching, foraging, and nesting, creating a sense of security and contentment. When designing the coop, nesting and perching areas must be properly assigned. Likewise, keeping the area free from predators and allowing the birds to roam and gather food all promote natural behavior and calm your furry friends.

## Reducing Stress

Providing ample space and enriching features reduces stress among birds. Stress leads to various health issues and negatively impacts the flock's overall quality of life. A well-designed space keeps your birds relaxed, makes them keen to explore the surroundings, and allows them to keep stress at bay.

### Behavioral Expression

No matter how many breeds you want to raise together, the design should always cater to the diverse behavioral needs of different bird species. Whether it's providing platforms for courtship, suitable nesting areas, or spaces for communal activities, fulfilling these design considerations allows birds to express their natural behaviors freely.

### Egg Quality

A comfortable and stress-free environment is crucial to consistent and quality egg production. Adequate spacing minimizes stress levels among birds, encouraging consistent egg laying. Thoughtful design includes strategically placed nesting boxes, ensuring easy access for hens, and reducing the likelihood of eggs being laid in undesirable locations. This contributes to improved egg quality, strong and durable shells, reduced contamination, and better hygiene.

### Reproductive Success

Properly designed nesting areas contribute to reproductive success. Nesting boxes or platforms should mimic the birds' instincts, encouraging successful egg-laying and raising their young.

### Encouraging Social Interaction

Well-designed habitats facilitate social interactions among birds. Socializing is crucial, especially for species that thrive in flocks. Communal spaces, perches, and designated areas for group activities contribute to a harmonious and socially engaged flock.

### Meat Quality

Regarding meat quality, a well-managed space is vital in ensuring healthy and robust poultry. Optimal spacing reduces aggressive behaviors, minimizing injuries and pecking incidents. Uninjured birds contribute to superior meat quality. Additionally, proper spacing ensures fair access to food, reducing competition among birds and promoting nutrient absorption. A stress-free environment positively influences the reproductive system, producing better meat quality. Overall, a well-designed space for poultry is integral to achieving optimal egg and meat quality, essential for the success and sustainability of poultry farming operations.

### Ventilation and Cleanliness

Proper ventilation is vital for maintaining a healthy environment. Well-designed habitats ensure good airflow, reducing the risk of respiratory issues. Furthermore, keeping cleaning and waste management in mind contributes to a hygienic space, minimizing the spread of diseases.

### Temperature Regulation

Adequate spacing and strategically placed elements in the habitat help regulate temperature. Birds are sensitive to extreme temperatures, and a well-designed habitat ensures they can find shelter, shade, or warmth as needed. Several factors, like using insulation material and controlling moisture, must be considered to achieve optimum temperature regulation. If several breeds are being raised in the same area, consider temperature zoning, where you designate zones in the coop according to age, and create microclimates feasible for each age group or breed.

### Preventing Diseases

Thoughtful design incorporates measures to prevent the spread of diseases. This includes spacing structures appropriately, isolating sick birds when necessary, and minimizing potential breeding grounds for parasites or pathogens. These spaces support healthy growth, reducing mortality and optimizing feed conversion rates.

The importance of a thoughtfully designed avian habitat cannot be overstated. This habitat goes beyond meeting basic shelter needs. It becomes a dynamic environment supporting a bird's life's physical, mental, and social aspects.

Creating spaces that align with their natural behaviors, encourage social interaction, and prioritize health considerations fosters an environment where birds can thrive, express themselves, and lead fulfilling lives. A well-designed avian haven is a testament to your commitment to the well-being of your feathered friends, ensuring a life of comfort, productivity, and health within their carefully crafted homes.

# Insulation for Temperature Regulation

## Maintaining Optimal Conditions

Adequate insulation is crucial to regulate temperatures within the poultry housing. Insulation helps maintain a stable environment, protecting birds from extreme heat or cold. This ensures optimal growth, egg production, and overall health.

### Preventing Heat Stress

In warmer climates, proper insulation prevents heat stress by minimizing the impact of external temperature fluctuations. It creates a more comfortable living space, reducing the poultry's risk of heat-related health issues.

### Addressing Cold Environments

During colder seasons, insulation retains heat within the structure, preventing drafts and ensuring that birds remain warm. This is vital for preventing frostbite and respiratory problems associated with exposure to low temperatures.

# The Use of Ventilation Systems

### Promoting Airflow

Adequate ventilation is essential for promoting airflow and maintaining fresh air within the poultry housing. Stagnant air can lead to the buildup of harmful gases, moisture, and airborne pathogens, negatively impacting the respiratory health of birds.

### Minimizing Respiratory Issues

Proper ventilation reduces the concentration of ammonia and other airborne pollutants. This minimizes the risk of respiratory issues, enhancing the overall respiratory health of the flock.

### Regulating Humidity Levels

Ventilation systems also play a role in regulating humidity levels. Controlling humidity is essential for preventing mold and bacteria growth, contributing to a healthier living environment for poultry.

# Predator-Proofing Measures

### Securing Outdoor Spaces

Designing outdoor areas with secure fencing and netting protects poultry from predators. Thoughtful design that incorporates secure fencing, buried hardware cloth, and reinforced structures is essential. Installing predator-resistant fencing, like hardware cloth with small mesh sizes, prevents access to small predators like raccoons and snakes. Burying the fencing material beneath the soil surface creates an additional barrier, deterring burrowing predators like foxes. Reinforcing structures, such as coops and roosts, with sturdy materials and locks further enhances protection.

Regular outdoor area maintenance and inspections are crucial to identify and promptly address potential vulnerabilities. Likewise, adequate lighting around the perimeter can also discourage nocturnal predators.

### Sturdy Construction

Ensure the poultry housing is constructed with sturdy materials and features secure locks. To begin, selecting durable materials resistant to weathering and wear is crucial. Thick and strong wood or metal provides a solid foundation, minimizing vulnerabilities that predators could exploit. Reinforcing vulnerable points, such as entry doors and windows, with additional locks or latches enhances security.

Moreover, paying attention to structural details is vital. Ensuring there are no gaps, cracks, or weak points in the construction eliminates potential predator entry points. Seal any openings with predator-resistant materials like hardware cloth with small mesh sizes.

### Elevated Roosts and Nesting Boxes

Elevating roosts and nesting boxes can deter ground-based predators. This reduces the risk of predation during vulnerable times, such as when birds are resting or laying eggs.

Creating an environment that caters to the specific needs of laying hens is fundamental for ensuring optimal egg-laying conditions. This next section delves into the intricacies of choosing suitable nesting materials, offering layout suggestions for nesting boxes, and implementing privacy measures to enhance the comfort of your hens during the egg-laying process.

# Choosing Suitable Nesting Materials

### Straw and Hay

Using straw or hay as nesting materials presents a multi-faceted advantage. These materials provide a soft and insulating bed for the hens to lay eggs. Straw and hay also absorb moisture effectively, ensuring a dry and comfortable environment conducive to egg-laying.

### Wood Shavings

Wood shavings are an excellent option for nesting material due to their absorbent nature. They create a clean and dry surface, minimizing the risk of eggs becoming soiled. It is crucial, however, to ensure that the wood shavings are free from sharp edges or splinters to prevent any harm to the hens.

### Nesting Pads or Mats

Pre-made nesting pads or mats, crafted from materials such as felt or rubber, offer a consistent and comfortable surface. These materials are easy to clean and maintain, contributing to a hygienic nesting space that promotes the overall well-being of the laying hens.

## Layout Suggestions for Nesting Boxes

### Consider Box Size

Thoughtful consideration of nesting box dimensions is pivotal. Boxes should be appropriately sized to ensure comfort for the hens. Boxes that are too large may inadvertently encourage multiple hens to share, potentially leading to broken eggs.

### Elevate Nesting Boxes

Elevating nesting boxes off the ground serves multiple purposes. Not only does it provide a sense of security for the hens, but it also minimizes the risk of them scratching and soiling the nesting materials. Elevated boxes reduce the chances of predation, creating a calm and secure environment for egg-laying.

### Adequate Number of Boxes

Providing an adequate number of nesting boxes is essential. Overcrowding can lead to competition for nesting spaces, causing stress among the hens and negatively impacting egg production. Having a sufficient number of boxes promotes a harmonious and stress-free environment.

## Ensuring Privacy for Optimum Egg-Laying Conditions

### Screening or Curtains

Implementing screening or curtains within the nesting area creates a private and secluded space. This privacy measure contributes to a sense of security for the hens, encouraging them to lay eggs undisturbed.

### Dim Lighting

Providing dim lighting in the nesting area caters to the hens' natural preferences. Hens favor dimly lit spaces for laying eggs, and this thoughtful design element contributes to a more relaxed egg-laying environment and reduces stress.

### Separate Laying Area

Designating a specific area for nesting separates it from other daily pursuits. This separation reduces disruptions and provides the hens with a quiet and dedicated space, further enhancing the overall comfort during the egg-laying process.

The nuances of nesting are crucial for creating an environment that prioritizes the comfort and well-being of laying hens. The meticulous choice of nesting materials, thoughtful layout suggestions, and the implementation of privacy measures collectively contribute to an atmosphere that maximizes productivity and fosters a stress-free and contented egg-laying process. By paying attention to these details with precision and care, you elevate the conditions for your poultry flock, ensuring that their nesting experience is characterized by comfort, security, and optimal well-being.

### Creating a Restful Environment

Creating a conducive roosting environment is crucial for your poultry's well-being and restful nights. You'll now be introduced to the necessity of appropriate roosting bars, height considerations, and spacing between roosts to provide optimal conditions for your birds' nightly repose.

# Appropriate Roosting Bars

### Material and Diameter

The choice of roosting bar material and diameter significantly influences your birds' comfort. Opt for materials that are comfortable for the hens to grip, such as smooth wood or PVC. The diameter of the roosting bars should be conducive to a secure grip, preventing foot problems like bumblefoot.

### Spacing and Placement

Proper spacing between roosting bars is essential. Aim for a distance that allows each bird enough space to perch comfortably without encroaching on the neighboring one's territory. Adequate spacing prevents overcrowding and minimizes the risk of aggressive behaviors.

### Adjustable vs. Fixed Bars

Consider the benefits of adjustable roosting bars, allowing you to modify the height as your birds grow or as you introduce new poultry to the flock. Fixed bars may limit flexibility, especially if you have a mixed-age flock.

# Height Considerations

## Natural Instincts

Chickens have a natural instinct to roost at higher elevations, mimicking their wild behavior of seeking elevated spots for safety during the night. Providing roosts at an appropriate height aligns with this instinct and promotes an overall sense of security for the birds.

### Avoiding Height Disparities

Maintain a consistent height for roosting bars within the coop. Avoid sharp disparities in height, as this can lead to hierarchy issues within the flock. A level roosting surface contributes to a harmonious and stress-free roosting experience.

### Accessibility for All Birds

Consider the accessibility of roosting bars for all birds, including those with physical limitations. If you have older or injured chickens, providing lower roosts ensures that every member of the flock can comfortably access their designated roosting spot.

# Preventing Overcrowding

Adequate spacing between roosts is vital for preventing overcrowding. Birds need personal space for comfort and to exhibit natural behaviors like preening and stretching. Sufficient space also minimizes the risk of injury caused by territorial disputes.

### Accommodating Different Breeds

Different chicken breeds have varying sizes and preferences when it comes to roosting. By offering varied spacing between roosts, you accommodate the diverse needs of your flock, ensuring that each bird can find a spot that suits them.

### Facilitating Easy Movement

The arrangement of roosts allows for easy movement within the coop. Birds should be able to navigate to and from their roosting spots without hindrance. This facilitates a stress-free bedtime routine for your poultry.

Understanding and implementing the realities of roosting contribute significantly to the overall well-being and restful nights of your flock. Appropriate roosting bars, careful height considerations, and thoughtfully spaced roosts ensure that each bird can enjoy a secure, comfortable, and stress-free roosting experience. By prioritizing these roosting realities, you create an environment that promotes the natural behaviors and instincts of your poultry, fostering a contented and harmonious coop atmosphere.

### Safeguarding Flocks from Disease

Biosecurity is a critical component of poultry management with the aim of preventing the introduction and spread of diseases within the flock and housing environment. By implementing stringent biosecurity measures, poultry farmers can enhance the overall health and productivity of their flocks. Here's an in-depth exploration of biosecurity practices:

### Perimeter Fencing

Establish a secure perimeter around the poultry housing facility using appropriate fencing. This prevents unauthorized access and reduces the risk of disease introduction by external sources, such as wild birds or animals.

### Controlled Access Points

Designate controlled access points for personnel, equipment, and visitors. Implement biosecurity protocols at these entry points, including foot baths, hand sanitization, and protective clothing, to minimize the risk of introducing contaminants.

### Quarantine Practices

Introduce a comprehensive quarantine system for new birds entering the flock. This involves isolating new additions for a specified period, allowing for observation and health checks to identify potential diseases before integration.

### Regular Health Monitoring

Implement regular health monitoring programs for the entire flock. This involves routine checks for signs of illness, monitoring feed and water consumption, and promptly addressing any abnormalities.

### Cleaning and Disinfection

Establish strict cleaning and disinfection protocols for equipment and vehicles entering the poultry facility. This prevents the transmission of pathogens on surfaces, reducing the risk of disease spread.

### Equipment Use

Designate specific equipment for use within the poultry facility whenever possible to avoid cross-contamination from other farming activities.

### Biosecurity Training

Provide comprehensive biosecurity training to everyone involved. This includes proper handling procedures, hygiene practices, and the importance of adhering to biosecurity protocols.

### Biosecurity Education

Educate staff, if you have any, on the potential risks associated with poultry diseases, emphasizing the role each individual plays in maintaining a bio-secure environment. Regular training sessions and updates are essential to reinforce these practices.

### Bird Netting and Deterrents

Install bird netting or deterrents to minimize contact between poultry and wild birds. Wild birds can carry diseases that pose a threat to domestic poultry, making it crucial to prevent direct or indirect interactions.

### Wildlife Management Plans

Develop and implement wildlife management plans to address potential threats from mammals that can transmit diseases. This may involve securing feed storage areas and implementing measures to discourage wildlife from entering the premises.

### Sustainable Practices in Poultry

Sustainability in poultry housing involves adopting practices that minimize environmental impact, promote resource efficiency, and contribute to the overall well-being of the flock. Here's an in-depth exploration of sustainable practices in poultry housing:

### Natural Lighting Solutions

Incorporate natural lighting solutions in poultry housing to reduce dependence on artificial lighting. This saves energy and promotes the well-being of birds as they respond positively to natural light cycles.

## Energy-Efficient Equipment

Invest in energy-efficient heating, ventilation, and cooling systems. This reduces energy consumption and operational costs while maintaining optimal environmental conditions within the poultry facility.

## Manure Management

Implement efficient manure management systems, such as composting or utilization as fertilizer. Proper disposal and recycling of manure contribute to soil health and minimize environmental impact.

## Recycling and Reusing Materials

Embrace recycling practices by reusing materials within the poultry housing structure. This includes repurposing materials like wood or metal for construction, reducing the need for new resources.

## Landscaping for Environmental Harmony

Incorporate landscaping around the poultry facility to enhance environmental harmony. This includes planting native vegetation, creating green spaces, and designing surroundings that support biodiversity.

## Water Conservation Practices

Implement water conservation practices, such as rainwater harvesting or the use of efficient watering systems. This minimizes water wastage and promotes responsible water usage within the poultry housing facility.

## Solar or Wind Power

Explore the feasibility of incorporating alternative energy sources, such as solar panels or wind turbines. Renewable energy contributes to sustainability by reducing reliance on traditional power grids.

## Energy-Efficient Heating Systems

Opt for energy-efficient heating systems that utilize renewable energy sources or advanced technologies to minimize energy consumption.

## Preserving Natural Habitats

Design poultry housing facilities with consideration for preserving natural habitats and biodiversity. Avoid encroaching on ecologically sensitive areas, and adopt designs that coexist harmoniously with the natural environment.

## Planting Hedgerows or Windbreaks

Planting hedgerows or windbreaks serves multiple purposes, including biodiversity preservation, wind protection, and creating microenvironments that benefit both poultry and wildlife.

## Feed and Bedding Procurement

Source poultry feed and bedding materials locally when possible, promoting sustainability in the supply chain. This reduces transportation-related carbon emissions and supports local economies.

## Sustainable Construction Materials

Use sustainable construction materials for building and maintaining poultry housing structures. This may include recycled or locally sourced materials with lower environmental impact.

Incorporating biosecurity measures and sustainable practices in poultry housing is essential to achieve a balance between ecology and productivity. Robust biosecurity safeguards flocks from diseases, ensuring a healthy and productive environment. Simultaneously, sustainable practices contribute to environmental stewardship, resource efficiency, and the long-term viability of poultry farming. By integrating these principles, farmers can create facilities that prioritize the well-being of the flock, minimize environmental impact, and promote overall sustainability in poultry management.

# Chapter 4: Feeding and Nutrition

Feeding and nutrition are at the heart of keeping poultry healthy and productive. If you want to protect your birds and guarantee safe and healthy products, you should pay attention to what you are feeding them. A balanced diet improves your birds' immunity and protects them from fungal, bacterial, and viral infections. It also makes their feathers look even nicer, improves their temperament, and enhances their well-being.

This chapter covers basic poultry nutrition, commercial feed components, and the benefits and potential hazards of treats and supplements.

# The Connection between a Balanced Diet and Optimal Bird Health

## FRUITS

Mango's
Kiwi
Papaya
Melons (no rind)
Berries
Pomegranates
Grapes
Cranberries
Banana's
Apples

## VEGGIES

Carrots (Tops Included)
Sweet Potatoes
Leafy Greens
Peppers, Assorted Colors
Green Beans
Sweet Peas
Sugar Snap Peas
Squash
Pumpkin
Corn

50-60% Of Diet Should Comprise
of Well-Balanced Pellets

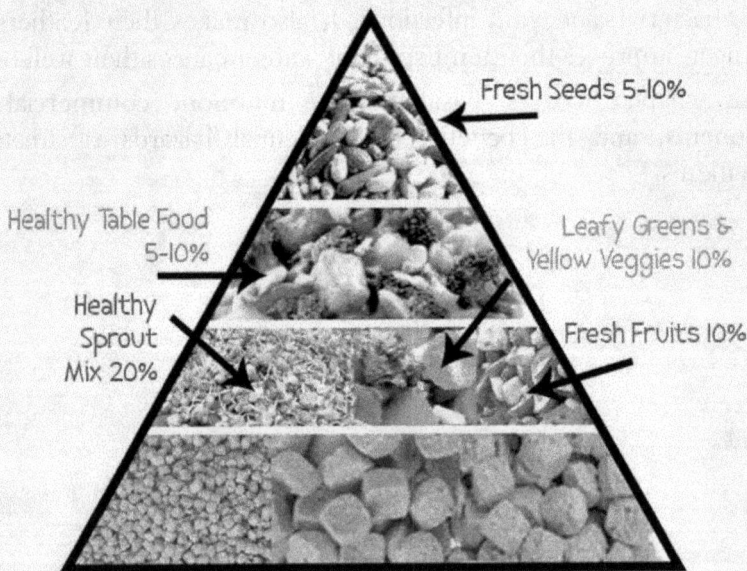

Fresh Seeds 5-10%

Healthy Table Food
5-10%

Leafy Greens &
Yellow Veggies 10%

Healthy
Sprout
Mix 20%

Fresh Fruits 10%

# AVIAN FOOD PYRAMID

Ⓝ Avocado's, Uncooked Beans, Chocolate, Alcohol, Caffiene, Shellfish & Undercooked Meat. Remove Fresh Foods After 2-3 hrs.

When people decide to raise poultry, they often plan in advance the type of bird they want to have and where they will raise their flock. However, many don't pay attention to poultry feed and just buy any high-quality brand without looking at the ingredients to check for chemicals or harmful additives. When you feed your birds with nutrient-rich food, they will be strong and energetic and produce high-quality eggs with disease-free chicks.

To get the most out of your birds, feed them a balanced diet from the start. A well-balanced diet greatly impacts their laying capacity, immune system, growth rate, and yolk sac utilization.

If you raise the birds for eggs and meat, you should feed them high amounts of fiber and protein to keep them full and increase the amount of good bacteria in their stomachs. Feed them food rich in vitamins to guarantee constant egg production, hatchability, healthy chicks, and good fertility. A poor diet reduces egg production, weakens the shells, and impacts the birds' overall health.

Feed plays a huge role in your birds' well-being and behavior. In fact, the right diet can revive a malnourished bird. Similar to human beings, if you are weak and lack energy, the doctor will recommend that you change your diet and start eating food high in protein, minerals, and fiber.

### Real Life Story

A young girl named Julia rescued a cute parrot and called it Lily. Sadly, Lily used to live in an abusive home, and her previous owners were negligent and didn't properly feed her. She was malnourished and severely underweight. Her feathers were falling off, and her organs were failing. Julia started feeding her seeds and fresh vegetables. However, the bird was still losing weight. So, she added pellets to Lily's diet with the seeds. Although Lily was eating the food, she remained underweight and malnourished for six months.

Julia was frustrated and wanted Lily to focus more on the pellets than the seeds. She removed the seeds from the diet and mainly put out pellets and vegetables. Lily started gaining weight and was feeling more energetic. However, her weight gain was slow. So, Julia decided to take her to the vet.

The vet recommended a type of high-quality organic food. Julia listened and only fed Lily the organic diet. After a couple of months, Lily gained weight and was full of energy. Her feathers looked better than ever, and she was finally happy.

It isn't an exaggeration to say that a well-balanced diet saved Lily's life. It turned her from a malnourished and sick bird who was on the verge of death to a full-of-life and joyful one.

# The Basics of Poultry Nutrition

Now that you understand the significance of feeding your birds a well-balanced diet, you are ready to discover the essential nutrients that will keep them healthy and protect them from diseases.

## Water

Water is necessary for transporting nutrients in birds' bodies, regulating their temperature, and keeping them hydrated. Make sure that your birds always have access to clean and fresh water. They should drink twice as much water as the amount of their feed.

## Protein

Proteins build body tissues like the beak, feathers, skin, cartilage, nerves, and muscles. They are also responsible for the birds' maintenance, development, and growth. Proteins are made of essential and non-essential amino acids. Birds' bodies can produce non-essential amino acids, but you should provide them with food rich in essential ones.

If you raise birds for eggs, give them food rich in protein like corn gluten, meat, fish, legumes, canola, or soybean.

Inadequate protein levels can cause many health issues and reduce egg and meat yield.

## Minerals

Minerals help bone and blood cell formulation, boost metabolism, activate enzymes, and prevent blood clotting. You should give your bird food high in zinc, selenium, manganese, iron, iodine, sodium, potassium, magnesium, chlorine, phosphorus, and calcium. Calcium improves bones and eggshell quality. Phosphorus boosts bone health, and chlorine increases the levels of hydrochloric acid, which aids in digestion. Potassium and sodium protect the nerves and muscles.

Birds require calcium during eggshell formation. They will use the calcium reserves in their skeletons if they don't receive enough. This can cause serious issues, and the hen will stop laying eggs.

### Vitamins

Make sure your birds get vitamin A to support their growth and development, vitamin D for eggshell formation, and vitamin B to increase energy levels and boost metabolism. Many of these vitamins can be given in the form of supplements. Others require external factors like vitamin D that can be produced by constant exposure to the sun.

### Energy

Ensure your birds consume enough calories daily to increase their energy levels and fuel all chemical reactions in their bodies.

Birds need energy for reproduction, digestion, maintenance, and growth. Luckily, almost all ingredients contain energy. If you want your birds to be more energetic, feed them corn, wheat, barley, meat, and fat.

### Fats

Fats are necessary for meat and poultry. They increase the birds' energy and boost their productivity.

### Carbohydrates

Carbohydrates boost the energy that fuels maintenance, growth, and daily activities. You should aim to strike a balance between carbs and fats in your birds' diet.

### Decoding Feed Labels

Like most bird or animal owners, you will mainly rely on commercial feed for your flock's meals. Commercial feed is store-bought food made specifically for poultry. There are many types to choose from; some are expensive brands that are made from high-quality ingredients, while others are lower quality and can contain harmful substances. Sometimes, high-quality brands are your best option since manufacturers usually test all ingredients in advance to guarantee their safety.

Before you choose a type of feed, check the components first to make sure it is made from healthy ingredients and doesn't contain harmful additives or chemicals.

# Commercial Feed Components

This section sheds light on all the common components you will find on commercial feed packages and what they mean.

## Cereal Grains

Cereal grains are dry grains and cereal by-products that sustain your poultry and boost their energy. There are usually different types of grains used in feed. In Asian countries, Brazil and the US use corn as the main ingredient and energy source. Canada, Europe, Russia, New Zealand, and Australia use wheat as the main source of poultry dietary energy. However, many manufacturers don't really focus on the nutritional benefits of the grain but make their choice based on its price. For instance, China and the US use wheat if it is cheaper. In Australia, they sometimes use sorghum instead of wheat. Sweden, Denmark, and Norway use rye and barley when grain prices are high.

Any changes manufacturers make to their products depend mainly on cost. That doesn't mean they should keep adding or removing ingredients whenever they feel like it. Any change, whether big or small, should be handled with caution. In fact, many manufacturers avoid making big changes to the feed components since they can cause digestive issues to the birds and reduce their productivity.

Different factors can impact the grains' quality, such as storage and seasonal conditions. If the grains aren't stored properly or grown in poor conditions, their energy content will reduce drastically. These conditions can also expose the grains to toxins or harmful organisms like fungi.

Environmental and genetic factors can also impact the quality of the grains and their nutritive value. These can make them hard to digest and cause serious issues for the birds.

Cereal by-products like rice bran and wheat bran are also used in the feed components.

## Protein Meals

Animal and vegetable proteins like fish, legumes, and oilseeds are used in poultry feed. Vegetable protein sources are usually the by-products of oilseed crops like sesame seed, linseed, peanut, copra, palm kernel, sunflower, canola, and soybean. They are made from the residue of the extracted oil. Similar to grain, countries also use different vegetable protein sources. Some use soybeans or sunflowers, and others use lupins, peas, or cottonseed. Manufacturers may use more than one vegetable resource if their prices are reasonable.

Animal protein sources used in poultry feed are feather meal, blood meal, poultry by-product meal, fish meal, meat meal, and meat and bone meal.

The animal industry has evolved in the last few years, and they have put more focus on increasing nutrient levels and improving the flavor.

Using animal resources in poultry feed can be challenging because a few people raise their concerns about it. Food safety has been put into question, with people worrying about recycling animal products and using them as feed ingredients. However, there haven't been any reports of birds getting sick. Some people were also worried that animal protein meals could cause Salmonella. It has been stated that harmful bacteria are usually destroyed through rendering, and recontamination is impossible. In most cases, birds get Salmonella through environmental factors instead of feed.

Animal protein meals contain high levels of amino acids and minerals and are also considered a source of energy.

Although there are some concerns surrounding animal protein meals, they have been incorporated into poultry feed for years. Using this ingredient is significant since it increases the economic and nutrient value of the feed and plays a role in producing high-quality meat and eggs.

### Fats and Oils

Fats and oils are often used in bird feed because they increase their energy and contain more nutrients than proteins and carbohydrates. They also contain fatty acids like linoleic acid. Various types of fats and oils, like cottonseed oil, palm oil, linseed oil, sunflower oil, canola oil, and soy oil, are used in poultry feed.

### Vitamins and Minerals

Minerals encourage development and normal growth in fowls. Feeds usually contain high levels of phosphorus and calcium, which increase egg production. You will also find other minerals like molybdenum, iodine, cobalt, selenium, zinc, manganese, iron, and copper. Lacking these minerals will cause health issues – and even death – for the birds.

The feeds also contain vitamins A, D, E, K, and B12, pantothenic acid, pyridoxine, thiamine, riboflavin, niacin, folic acid, choline, and biotin, which promote the bird's well-being and improve their health.

### Additives

Additives enhance feed qualities, improve the bird's digestion, productivity, growth, and health, and prevent disease.

## Antioxidants

Fat is usually added to bird feeds, especially in fish meals. However, products high in fats are at risk of going bad. To protect the feed and give it a long shelf life, manufacturers add antioxidants.

## Antibiotics

There are microbes and bad bacteria in the digestive tract of all animals and birds. This bacteria can cause serious health issues, like damaging the intestines. Adding antibiotics to the feed will eliminate the bad bacteria and keep the bird protected from infections.

## Antibiotic Alternatives

Some people are against the use of antibiotics because they eliminate the good bacteria as well. This is why manufacturers have developed and used alternatives that kill bad bacteria and increase the number of good ones.

## Free-Flowing Agents

The feed should flow easily in the feeders so it doesn't get stuck and leave the birds hungry. Manufacturers add free-flowing agents to prevent the feeds from packing down. These agents don't react with any of the ingredients.

## Coccidiostats

Coccidiosis is a parasitic disease that infects birds' intestine tracts. It isn't serious if the coccidia is at low levels. At high levels, this condition can kill your poultry. Adding coccidiostats to the feed will prevent the parasite from spreading and boost their immune system.

Coccidiostats isn't a treatment. It only provides protection.

## Pelleting Additives

Pelleting additives are added to the feed to enhance its efficiency and ensure the ingredients are packed together in small pellets so the bird can eat them with ease.

## Mold Inhibitors

Cereals can be infected with mold during harvesting, processing, or storing. Even though the mold can be removed, it will still release mycotoxins, which can be fatal to the poultry. Mold inhibitors prevent contamination and mold growth.

### Feeding Enzymes

Some of the ingredients used in poultry feed have anti-nutritional properties, rendering them useless. Feeding enzymes can break down these properties to increase the potential of alternative grains.

### Quality Indicators

Naturally, you want to get the best quality feed for your poultry. You may think that the most expensive or popular brands are the safest option. However, this isn't always the case. There are simple things you can do to guarantee you are getting the best feed for your birds.

- Look at the ingredients and make sure they contain proteins, carbohydrates, vitamins, minerals, fats, and grains.
- Check to see the additives they are using and make sure they haven't added any toxic or harmful chemicals.
- Read the feed preview online and see what other people are saying.
- Smell it before using it. If it has a strange odor, it probably isn't high-quality.

# Supplements and Treats

If your birds are suffering from vitamin deficiency, you may want to give them supplements to boost their energy and improve their strength. You still shouldn't give them something that can affect their eggs, meat, or health.

### Advantages of Using Supplements for Poultry

- Improve digestion
- Aid in absorbing nutrients from feed
- Boost the immune system
- Reduce infection
- Protect against diseases
- Increase egg production and quality
- Improve growth rate
- Strengthen bones
- Keep poultry active
- Enhance laying duration
- Improve overall health

### Potential Hazards of Using Supplements for Poultry

- They aren't substitutes for nutrients
- They increase antimicrobial resistance
- Expose the poultry to harmful amounts of endotoxins, which can impact your health as well.

You love your poultry, and you probably want to spoil them every now and then. Giving them treats will make them happy and improve their mood, especially if they have been stressed. Just like supplements, there are advantages and disadvantages to treats.

### Benefits of Using Treats

- Boost birds' immune system
- Add minerals and vitamins to their diet
- Boost their mood
- Improve their behavior

### Potential Hazards of Giving Poultry Treats

- It can inadvertently replace nutritious food
- Obesity
- Reduce egg production
- Feather picking

Heart issues Give your poultry healthy snacks to avoid these potential hazards:

- Oatmeal
- Cottage cheese
- Pasta and noodles
- Mealworms
- Corn
- Ginger
- Watermelon
- Pumpkin
- Meat

# Natural Foraging for Backyard Poultry

Natural foraging is letting your birds fetch their food by themselves. Many farmers prefer to let their animals wander around and search for food. Before you make a decision about backyard foraging, consider its advantages and disadvantages.

Natural foraging is letting your birds fetch their food by themselves.

## Advantages of Natural Foraging

- Environmentally friendly
- You give back to the environment
- You give your birds the chance to be out in nature, get fresh air, and be exposed to the sun, which is a natural source of Vitamin D
- The chickens become more sustainable
- Reduces the number of insects
- They will get animal proteins and Vitamin B from eating those insects
- Foraging is better and healthier than commercial feed as the birds will consume more saturated fats and vitamins
- It is more cost-effective since you won't have to buy commercial food
- Your poultry will have the chance to socialize with other birds
- It is great exercise for them and prevents them from gaining weight

- Keeps your birds active
- Eggs will be more nutritious

**Potential Hazards of Natural Foraging**

- Your poultry will be easy prey for predators
- They will make big holes while searching for food, which prevents the grass from regrowing
- Poultry that forage will make a mess by discharging wherever
- The birds are at risk of inhaling or ingesting harmful substances
- They will eat anything from your garden, including potting plants and flowers
- You will struggle to find the eggs since they can lay them anywhere they can reach

If you want to raise healthy poultry and consume their eggs and meat, you should pay close attention to what you are feeding them. One small mistake can make your birds sick and affect their products. Remember, you also love these funny, feathery creatures, so protect them and help them stay healthy by making sure their feed is highly nutritious.

Before buying commercial food, read the ingredient list on the package thoroughly. Make sure there are no harmful chemicals or additives that can harm your poultry. Check the expiration date as well; expired products are dangerous and often lack proper nutrients.

Whether you want to let your poultry forage or not is your choice. You just need to consider the advantages and disadvantages very well before making a decision.

# Chapter 5: Poultry Health and Wellness

The health and wellness of poultry are intricately connected to proactive care and the early detection of ailments. This relationship is pivotal in enhancing your birds' longevity and productivity. By adopting a vigilant and preemptive approach to poultry health, caretakers can address potential issues before they escalate, safeguarding the flock's well-being and optimizing their performance.

The health and wellness of poultry are intricately connected to proactive care and the early detection of ailments.

Proactive care involves a comprehensive regimen that encompasses preventive measures, regular health assessments, and a keen awareness of the environmental factors impacting the birds. This proactive approach sets the foundation for early detection, where subtle signs of illness or distress can be identified before they manifest into severe health issues.

Early detection, in turn, becomes a linchpin for maintaining the longevity and productivity of poultry. Detecting illnesses in their nascent stages allows for timely intervention, reducing the severity and duration of the ailment. This guarantees the individual well-being of each bird and prevents the spread of diseases within the flock. Moreover, addressing health concerns early on minimizes the impact on the overall productivity of poultry, allowing them to continue contributing to egg production, meat quality, or other desired outcomes.

Implementing a proactive healthcare strategy means arranging regular health check-ups and vaccination programs, maintaining optimal living conditions, and always giving a prompt response to any behavioral changes or symptoms observed. Caretakers who adopt these practices establish a robust foundation for sustained poultry health and, consequently, prolonged periods of productivity.

In essence, the intrinsic link between proactive care, early detection of ailments, and the longevity and productivity of birds underscores the importance of a holistic and vigilant approach to poultry health and wellness. Prioritizing these aspects contributes to the entire flock's collective resilience and efficiency, ultimately fostering a thriving and sustainable poultry environment.

# Common Poultry Diseases

Poultry diseases can pose significant challenges to the health and productivity of your flock. Understanding the characteristics of common diseases is essential for early detection and effective management.

### Coccidiosis

**Causative Agent:** Protozoan parasites (Eimeria spp.).

**Symptoms:** Bloody diarrhea, lethargy, decreased feed intake, and reduced weight gain.

**Prevention:** Maintain clean and dry bedding to reduce oocyst survival, provide medicated feed containing coccidiostats, and practice strict biosecurity.

**Treatment:** Administer anticoccidial medications as prescribed by a veterinarian. Supportive care includes maintaining hydration and proper nutrition.

### Real-Life Recovery Story

Emma's farm included vibrant and spirited broiler chickens. One morning, Emma noticed that a few chickens from her flock had their feathers ruffled, and their eyes looked dull and weary. Recognizing the urgency of the situation, Emma decided to investigate further. She noticed a concerning sign – the droppings were tinged with blood, confirming the symptom of bloody diarrhea. Fear gripped Emma's heart as she remembered stories of farm owners sharing their stories of chickens succumbing to the notorious coccidiosis.

Without wasting a moment, Emma isolated the suspected chickens and reached out to a trusted veterinarian,

The vet confirmed the presence of an infective parasite causing coccidiosis and tailored a treatment plan for the isolated chicken. In a week, the feathers started regaining their luster and became completely healthy at the end of the treatment. This story highlights the importance of keen observation, prompt intervention, and seeking professional help to ensure the well-being of your feathered friends.

### Holistic Solutions

Beyond medication, holistic approaches include maintaining a clean and dry environment, providing balanced nutrition, and regular check-ups. Daisy's recovery highlights how a holistic strategy can contribute to overall well-being.

### Infectious Bronchitis

**Causative Agent:** Avian coronavirus.

**Symptoms:** Respiratory distress, coughing, sneezing, and decreased egg production.

**Prevention:** Implement vaccination programs, practice strict biosecurity measures to limit exposure, and isolate new birds. Adequate ventilation in coops is essential.

**Treatment:** Supportive care to manage respiratory symptoms. Antibiotics may be prescribed in severe cases under veterinary guidance.

### Real-Life Recovery Story

In a coop nestled on a countryside farm, the coop owner (Ben) found himself hearing raspy coughs from a hen. He ignored the sound and went to work on his daily farm duties. However, in a few days, the entire flock started producing the same cough sound. Recognizing the urgency, Ben immediately contacted one of his friends who was raising livestock poultry himself. His friend, Alex, advised Ben to isolate the birds that were actively coughing and seemed in distress.

The vet was called in to run diagnostic tests, which confirmed the development of infective bronchitis in the flock. The second thing Alex noticed was the high levels of humidity, which is an aggravating factor in the spread of bronchitis within the flock. Targeted vaccination was advised by the vet, whereas the design of the coop was changed to convert it into a ventilation coop to reduce humidity and limit the exposure to other birds in the flock.

In a matter of weeks, the once somber coop transformed into a bustling haven again, and the hens went back to their egg-laying routine. As advised by the vet, Ben continued to uphold a robust health management plan, ensuring the well-being of the flock for years to come.

### Holistic Solutions

Aside from vaccination, holistic care involves clean habitats, optimal nutrition, and mental stimulation. Charlie's recovery highlights the need for a holistic approach to combat respiratory diseases.

### Newcastle Disease

**Causative Agent:** Avian paramyxovirus type 1.

**Symptoms:** Respiratory distress, nervous system disorders, and a drop in egg production.

**Prevention:** Vaccinate against Newcastle disease, implement strict biosecurity measures, and properly dispose of infected carcasses.

**Treatment:** There is no specific cure. Focus on supportive care. Euthanasia may be considered in severe cases.

### Holistic Solution

A holistic approach includes clean environments, balanced nutrition, and regular mental stimulation. This showcases the resilience achieved through a comprehensive health strategy.

## Avian Influenza

**Causative Agent:** Influenza A virus.

**Symptoms:** Respiratory distress, swollen heads, and a sudden drop in egg production.

**Prevention:** Strict biosecurity practices, surveillance for early detection, and vaccination in high-risk areas.

**Treatment:** Supportive care. Culling may be necessary to prevent the disease from spreading in severe cases.

### Real-Life Recovery Story

In a cozy backyard lived a cheerful rooster with a few hens and their caring owner, Charlie. One day, the rooster started acting strange – breathing heavily, having a swollen head, and looking a bit tired. Charlie knew something was wrong and remembered reading about avian influenza.

Worried about the rooster, Charlie quickly reached out to the local vet. The veterinarian advised moving the rooster to an isolated space, separate from the rest of the birds, and suggested an antiviral treatment. In a matter of days, the antiviral treatment and the care Charlie provided enabled the rooster to recover in no time to crow and greet the day again. Immediate isolation, administering the right treatment, and providing the required care enable most poultry birds to recover unless it's a terminal illness or a life-threatening disease.

### Holistic Solutions

Beyond medication, holistic strategies include maintaining strict biosecurity to prevent viral spread. Proper ventilation and hygiene in the coop, alongside a balanced diet, supports overall flock health. Oliver's recovery underscores the role of vaccination and regular health checks in preventing future outbreaks.

### Fowl Pox

**Causative Agent:** Avian poxvirus.

**Symptoms:** Skin and mucous membrane lesions, reduced feed intake, and a drop in egg production.

**Prevention:** Vaccination and mosquito control are necessary to prevent transmission and isolation of infected birds.

**Treatment:** Supportive care. Recovery is generally spontaneous, but isolation is crucial to preventing its spread.

### Real-Life Recovery Story

Meet Rosie, a friendly hen who faced fowl pox and survived. The hen was raised by a family but was abandoned due to unfortunate circumstances. Sam brought Rosie home from an animal shelter, adding the hen to his backyard coop. Within a week, the hen started developing lesions on the wattles and comb. Sam immediately recognized the lesions as some birds in his flock had already been affected by fowl pox and recovered after adequate management.

After isolating the hen, Sam gently cleaned the lesions and applied the topical ointment recommended by the vet. He also ensured Rosie ate nutritious treats to keep her strength up. Over time, the pox started to fade away, and the hen recovered within a few days. Sam's quick actions and caring efforts made all the difference. It's a reminder that with a little understanding and some tender care, anyone can help their feathered friends bounce back from challenges like fowl pox and keep the whole flock healthy.

### Holistic Solutions

Holistic measures involve mosquito control, as mosquitoes transmit the flupox virus. This underscores the significance of a well-balanced, vitamin-rich diet to boost the immune system. Regular coop cleaning and avoiding overcrowding contribute to preventing fowlpox in the flock.

### Marek's Disease

**Causative Agent:** Marek's disease virus (herpesvirus).

**Symptoms:** Paralysis, weight loss, and the development of tumors.

**Prevention:** Vaccination of day-old chicks, strict biosecurity measures, and maintaining a virus-free environment.

**Treatment:** There is no cure for this. Focus on supportive care. Euthanasia may be considered for affected birds.

### Holistic Solutions

Holistic strategies include genetic selection for resistance to Marek's disease and maintaining stress-free environments. Max's recovery underscores the role of nutrition in supporting the immune system. Regular flock health assessments and vaccination protocols are essential for preventing Marek's disease.

## Respiratory Diseases

**Causative Agents:** Mycoplasma, infectious Coryza.

**Symptoms:** Sneezing, nasal discharge, coughing, and swollen sinuses.

**Prevention:** Practice strict biosecurity, vaccination against respiratory diseases, and maintain optimal living conditions with proper ventilation.

**Treatment:** Antibiotics prescribed by a veterinarian based on diagnostic tests.

### Real-Life Recovery Story

In a suburban backyard, Ruby, a spirited backyard hen, caught a menacing respiratory infection. It started with subtle signs – a hint of lethargy and a change in the melodic clucks. Ruby's owner, Sara, noticed nasal discharge and swollen sinuses near the beak, and the tone of clucks had changed – plus, Ruby showed clear signs of feeling tired throughout the day. Swiftly, Sara sought the expertise of Dr. Anderson, the local avian veterinarian. Early diagnosis revealed a respiratory infection that threatened Ruby's well-being and could potentially affect the entire backyard flock. Dr. Anderson recommended immediate isolation to curb the spread and initiated a targeted antibiotic treatment to combat the infection.

With each passing day, the antibiotic treatment worked its magic, and the sparkle returned to Ruby's eyes. The once-muted clucks transformed into joyful sounds echoing through the backyard. This tale of Ruby underlines the critical role of quick intervention, expert guidance, and a vigilant owner in overcoming respiratory challenges in backyard poultry.

### Holistic Solutions

Holistic approaches involve proper ventilation, minimizing dust and ammonia levels, and reducing stress. Ruby's recovery underscores the importance of nutrition in supporting respiratory health. Regular cleaning and disinfection of the coop contribute to preventing respiratory diseases.

## External Parasites

**Causative Agents:** Mites, lice.

**Symptoms:** Feather loss, irritation, decreased egg production.

**Prevention:** Regularly clean the coop and nesting areas, provide dust baths, and treat affected birds promptly.

**Treatment:** Use insecticides and acaricides as recommended by a veterinarian. Implement preventive measures to avoid reinfestation.

### Real-Life Recovery Story

Max, an animal activist living in Mexico, rescued a rooster from a cockfighting match. Unfortunately, the rooster had already fought in cockfighting matches and was carrying several cuts and bruises. Max brought the rooster to his home to attend to the injuries. Within a few days, the rooster started recovering and regaining strength.

Max already had a pair of playful labradors he rescued recently. Although the friendly pet dogs welcomed the new feathered friend, they were suffering from a mite infestation, which ultimately made its way to the rooster's feathers.

Recognizing the urgency, Max started cleaning the rooster cage, removing any potential hiding spots for the pesky intruders. Armed with an appropriate parasite treatment recommended by the local veterinarian, Max nursed the rooster back to health.

As the days passed, the feathers regained their luster, and his crowing echoed triumphantly through the coop once more. This tale highlights the necessity of regular inspections, quick intervention, and a vigilant owner in maintaining the well-being of poultry birds.

### Holistic Solutions

Holistic measures include maintaining a clean coop, dust baths, and using natural remedies to repel parasites. Percy's recovery underscores the importance of providing a stress-free environment. Regular parasite prevention protocols contribute to overall flock well-being.

### Intestinal Worms

**Causative Agents:** Roundworms, tapeworms.

**Symptoms:** Weight loss, decreased egg production, diarrhea.

**Prevention:** Regular deworming programs, maintaining clean living conditions, and preventing access to contaminated areas.

**Treatment:** Administer anthelmintic medications as prescribed by a veterinarian based on fecal examinations.

### Real-Life Recovery Story

Sammy is a livestock farmer who loves raising free-range chickens. Although the flock was well-fed and taken care of, a few hens from the flock seemed lethargic. In the next few days, the egg production decreased, persuading Sammy to isolate the hens and take them to the vet for a health check. The vet suggested monitoring the birds and running a diagnostic test for parasite infestation on fecal samples Sammy brought for testing.

The diagnosis confirmed the wormy woes, and a deworming treatment was prescribed to send those intruders packing. But that wasn't all; Sammy cleaned the coop, inspected the free-range area for worm infestations, and added a special menu to boost the immune system. As the days went by, Sammy's free-range chicken became more spirited than ever - thanks to the vet's expert advice and adequate care!

### Holistic Solutions

Holistic measures include rotational grazing and maintaining a clean environment to reduce worm exposure. Sammy's recovery underscores the role of a well-balanced diet in supporting the immune system. Regular deworming protocols and monitoring contribute to overall intestinal health.

### Egg Drop Syndrome (EDS)

**Causative Agent:** Avian adenovirus.

**Symptoms:** Drop in egg production, soft-shelled or misshapen eggs, and reproductive tract disorders.

**Prevention:** Biosecurity measures, vaccination, and proper management of breeding flocks.

**Treatment:** There is no specific treatment. Focus on preventing the spread through vaccination.

### Real-Life Recovery Story

Ella, a layer hen, was the first in the flock to produce eggs but suddenly developed the mysterious egg drop syndrome. While every layer hen was taken care of, Ella got special attention as her egg production stopped, making the owner, Jenna, concerned. She took the hen for a vet health checkup, but no definitive diagnosis was made. A few days later, Ella laid a soft-shelled egg – a telltale sign pointing toward egg drop syndrome (something the vet had mentioned on the previous visit).

As there was no specific treatment for the syndrome, Jenna started researching it to create an effective management plan. She prepared a stress-free corner of the farm for Ella with a few special treats to make her comfortable and help her release any stress. Jenna religiously cared for Ella for several days, and at last, the hen started laying eggs again!

### Holistic Solutions

Holistic approaches involve stress reduction through proper management practices. Ella's recovery underscores the significance of providing a well-balanced diet to support egg production. Regular health assessments and preventive measures contribute to sustained egg quality.

### Botulism

**Causative Agent:** Clostridium botulinum toxin.

**Symptoms:** Weakness, paralysis, drooping wings, and difficulty in breathing.

**Prevention:** Ensure clean water sources, proper carcass disposal, and avoid stagnant water.

**Treatment:** Antitoxin administration and supportive care.

### Holistic Solutions

Holistic approaches involve preventing access to contaminated water sources. Benny's recovery underscores the role of maintaining a clean environment and providing proper nutrition. Regular water source monitoring and preventive measures contribute to botulism prevention.

### Erysipelas

**Causative Agent:** Erysipelothrix rhusiopathiae bacteria.

**Symptoms:** Swollen wattles, joints, and lameness.

**Prevention:** Sanitation, vaccination, and controlling exposure to infected environments.

**Treatment:** Antibiotics prescribed by a veterinarian.

### Holistic Solutions

Holistic measures involve strict biosecurity to prevent the introduction of the bacterium-causing erysipelas. Emily's recovery underscores the significance of a well-balanced diet and stress reduction. Regular health checks and vaccinations contribute to erysipelas prevention.

### Fatty Liver Hemorrhagic Syndrome (FLHS)

**Causative Factor:** Excessive fat accumulation in the liver.

**Symptoms:** Sudden death, pale comb, and hemorrhages in liver tissues.

**Prevention:** Balanced nutrition, especially for laying hens, and preventing obesity.

**Treatment:** Adjusting the diet and providing supportive care.

**Holistic Solutions**

Holistic approaches involve providing a well-balanced diet with appropriate energy levels. Freddie's recovery underscores the role of stress reduction in preventing fatty liver hemorrhagic syndrome. Regular monitoring and dietary adjustments contribute to overall liver health.

## Ascites (Water Belly)

**Causative Factors:** Heart or lung issues leading to fluid accumulation in the abdomen.

**Symptoms:** Abdominal swelling, difficulty breathing, and decreased activity.

**Prevention:** Proper ventilation, balanced nutrition, and maintaining optimal environmental conditions.

**Treatment:** Addressing underlying causes, diuretics, and supportive care.

**Holistic Solutions**

Holistic measures involve managing growth rates and providing an appropriate diet. Alice's recovery underscores the significance of controlling environmental factors like temperature and ventilation. Regular monitoring and preventive measures contribute to ascites prevention.

## Gout

**Causative Factors:** Kidney dysfunction leading to uric acid accumulation.

**Symptoms:** Swollen joints, lameness, and visceral gout affecting internal organs.

**Prevention:** Providing a balanced diet and maintaining proper hydration.

**Treatment:** Addressing underlying Gout.

**Holistic Solutions**

Holistic approaches involve providing a well-balanced diet with controlled protein levels. George's recovery underscores the role of stress reduction and maintaining proper hydration. Regular monitoring and dietary adjustments contribute to gout prevention.

## Infectious Bursal Disease (Gumboro)

**Causative Agent:** Infectious bursal disease virus.

**Symptoms:** Immunosuppression, bursal atrophy, and increased susceptibility to other diseases.

**Prevention:** Vaccination, biosecurity measures, and proper management practices.

**Treatment:** No specific treatment; focus on prevention through vaccination.

Regular veterinary consultation and a comprehensive health management plan are essential components of maintaining a healthy flock.

### Holistic Solutions

Holistic measures involve maintaining strict biosecurity and vaccination protocols. Isabella's recovery underscores the role of providing a stress-free environment and balanced nutrition. Regular health checks and preventive measures contribute to IBD prevention.

# Maintaining a Healthy Flock

### Biosecurity

Biosecurity measures play a key role in preventing the introduction and spread of diseases. This involves controlling access to the poultry area, disinfecting equipment, and isolating new birds before introducing them to the flock.

### Vaccinations

Vaccination is a key preventive measure. Establish a vaccination program tailored to the prevalent diseases in your region. Regular consultation with a veterinarian is vital for developing an effective vaccination schedule.

### Clean and Dry Environment

Maintaining a clean and dry environment is essential for reducing the risk of disease transmission. Regular cleaning and disinfection of the coop, along with proper waste management, can minimize the buildup of pathogens.

### Nutritional Management

Proper nutrition is fundamental for a strong immune system. Provide a well-balanced and nutritionally rich diet for your poultry to support overall health and reduce susceptibility to diseases.

### Quarantine New Birds

Isolating new birds for a period before introducing them to the existing flock is a critical biosecurity measure. This prevents the introduction of potential pathogens and allows for the early detection of any underlying health issues.

### Monitoring and Early Intervention

Regular monitoring of the flock for signs of illness is essential. Early detection allows for prompt intervention, minimizing the impact of diseases on the overall health and productivity of the poultry. Establishing a close relationship with a poultry veterinarian enables timely and effective responses to emerging health challenges.

By diligently implementing these preventive measures and tailoring them to the specific needs of your flock, you can create a resilient and thriving poultry environment that contributes to the longevity and productivity of your birds. Regular veterinary consultations and ongoing education about local disease challenges are key components of successful poultry health management.

### Proactive Care

Maintaining a healthy flock extends beyond medical interventions. Proactive care involves a multifaceted approach, emphasizing cleanliness, quarantine practices, and regular inspections as crucial components in preventing diseases and ensuring the overall well-being of poultry.

# Cleanliness

## Importance of Clean Coops

**Clean living environments are paramount for preventing the spread of diseases.**
*https://unsplash.com/photos/brown-hen-on-brown-wooden-fence-ej5XXS8_2B8*

Clean living environments are paramount for preventing the spread of diseases. Regularly clean and disinfect coops, nesting areas, and feeding equipment to eliminate potential sources of contamination. This reduces the risk of bacterial and parasitic infections, fostering a healthier environment for your flock.

### Effective Waste Management

Proper waste management is integral to maintaining cleanliness. Promptly remove droppings and spilled feed to decrease the risk of pathogens. A well-managed waste system mitigates the risk of diseases associated with bacterial and parasitic contamination.

### Hygiene Practices

Practicing personal hygiene when handling poultry is equally important. Wash your hands thoroughly after interacting with the flock to prevent the unintentional transmission of pathogens. Regularly clean equipment and tools to avoid cross-contamination.

# Quarantine Practices

## Purpose of Quarantine

Quarantine serves as protection against the introduction of diseases. When introducing new birds to the flock, isolate them for a specific period. This allows you to monitor for any signs of illness without jeopardizing the health of the flock. Quarantine is especially crucial when adding poultry from different sources.

### Observation Period

During the quarantine period, observe new birds closely for any illness symptoms. Common signs may include lethargy, respiratory distress, or changes in droppings. This cautious approach prevents the potential introduction of diseases that might otherwise go unnoticed.

### Biosecurity Measures

Integrate biosecurity measures into quarantine practices. Limit access to quarantined birds, use separate equipment, and change clothing between handling different groups. This minimizes the risk of disease transmission between quarantined and established flock members.

# Regular Inspections

## Importance of Regular Check-Ups

Regular inspections play a pivotal role in disease prevention. Schedule routine check-ups for your flock conducted by a veterinarian. These can lead to the early detection of potential health issues, enabling timely intervention and preventing the escalation of diseases.

### Signs of Good Health

Familiarize yourself with the signs of good health in poultry. Active behavior, glossy plumage, bright eyes, and normal droppings are indicators of a healthy bird. Identifying deviations from these norms gives you the chance to act as soon as possible.

### Environmental Assessments

Regularly assess environmental conditions such as ventilation, lighting, and temperature. Make sure these factors align with optimal poultry health. A well-maintained environment reduces stress and boosts the flock's immune system.

Incorporating these proactive care practices into your poultry management routine creates a robust foundation for disease prevention. Beyond relying solely on medications, a holistic approach that prioritizes cleanliness, quarantine measures, and regular inspections is key to sustaining a healthy and thriving flock. Regular consultation with a veterinarian further enhances your ability to tailor these practices to the specific needs of your poultry.

# Mental Well-Being and Stimulation for Poultry

Maintaining the mental well-being of your poultry is crucial for a healthy and happy flock. Introducing toys, foraging activities, and environmental enrichment can keep them mentally engaged, reduce stress, and promote overall welfare.

### Pecking Balls

**Purpose:** Provides entertainment and encourages natural pecking behavior.

**Benefits:** Reduces boredom, frustration, and aggressive pecking.

**Types:** Hanging pecking balls.

### Mirror Toys

**Purpose:** Reflective surfaces stimulate curiosity and social interaction.

**Benefits:** Reduces loneliness and promotes socialization.

**Types:** Mirrors placed strategically in the coop or run.

### Swinging Perches

**Purpose:** Mimic natural movements, offering physical and mental stimulation.

**Benefits:** Engages birds in balancing activities, promoting agility.

**Types:** Hanging perches or swings within the coop.

### Scatter Feeding

**Purpose:** Encourage natural foraging behaviors.

**Benefits:** Reduces stress, stimulates mental activity, and prevents boredom.

**Types:** Scatter grains or seeds around the area for birds to peck.

### Hanging Vegetables

**Purpose:** Provide a challenging foraging experience.

**Benefits:** Promotes physical activity and mental engagement.

**Types:** Hang vegetables, such as cabbage or lettuce, for birds to peck.

### Dust Bath Areas

**Purpose:** Facilitate natural dust bathing behavior.

**Benefits:** Aids in feather maintenance and reduces stress.

**Types:** Create dedicated areas with dust or sand for birds to bathe.

### Vegetation and Hideouts

**Purpose:** Create a dynamic environment with hiding spots.

**Benefits:** Mimics a natural setting, reducing stress and promoting exploration.

**Types:** Plant vegetation or add shelters like wooden boxes.

### Perches and Platforms

**Purpose:** Offer elevated spaces for roosting and observation.

**Benefits:** Birds feel secure, and it provides opportunities for mental stimulation.

**Types:** Install wooden perches or raised platforms.

### Colorful Objects

**Purpose:** Introduce visual stimulation.

**Benefits:** Adds variety to the environment, reducing monotony.

**Types:** Hang colorful objects, like cloth strips or shiny materials.

### Considerations for Implementation:

#### Safety First

- Make sure that all enrichments are safe and free from sharp edges or toxic materials.

#### Rotation of Items

- Regularly rotate or introduce new toys and enrichments to maintain interest.

#### Observation

- Monitor how birds interact with enrichments to gauge preferences.

#### Adapt to Seasons

- Adjust enrichments based on weather conditions to guarantee year-round suitability.

Integrating these mental stimulation strategies into your poultry management practices leads to a more enriched and content flock. Happy and mentally engaged birds are more likely to exhibit natural behavior, experience reduced stress, and contribute to a healthier overall environment. Regular observation and adaptation to the preferences of your specific flock enhances the effectiveness of these initiatives.

# Chapter 6: Breeding and Incubation

Breeding and incubation in poultry are complex processes, and each egg symbolizes the promise of a new beginning. Exploring the science of fertility provides an intricate understanding of the processes governing the journey from mating to hatchling. This chapter invites you to navigate a comprehensive journey where the art of caregiving converges with the science of life, creating life from egg to hatchling in meticulous detail.

## From Egg to Hatchling

Breeding and incubation represent a profound journey where the caretaker becomes a witness to the unfolding miracle of life. Observing the metamorphosis of a seemingly ordinary egg into a lively hatchling establishes a connection that goes beyond the routine, adding an element of wonder to each step in the process.

The Enigmatic Nature of Incubation

This marks the initiation of a profound bond between caretakers and the potential hatchlings.
*https://unsplash.com/photos/person-holding-brown-and-black-bird-6G0HWfLvP4Y*

Incubation is a process that combines anticipation with the miracle of development. It involves carefully managing the warmth required for eggs to hatch, accompanied by the rhythmic pulsation of life within. This marks the initiation of a profound bond between caretakers and the potential hatchlings. To become familiar with the enigmatic nature of incubation, here's a real-life example depicting its power.

In a rustic farm nestled in the hills, Joe meticulously managed his incubator, a treasure trove of potential life. One brisk morning, as he checked the eggs, he discovered a surprise—a tiny quail egg tucked among the chicken eggs. The quail, oblivious to the mix-up, hatched alongside its larger companions. The farmer, amused by this unexpected addition, marveled at the unpredictability of life and the surprises each incubation cycle could bring.

# Factors Shaping Breeding Success

Breeding success is contingent on numerous interacting factors. The health and genetic makeup of the breeding pair, environmental conditions, and nutritional considerations collectively influence the outcome of the journey from egg to hatchling. A nuanced understanding of these factors empowers poultry keepers to optimize conditions, ensuring a fruitful breeding experience.

# Incubation Process and Milestones

## Pre-Incubation

### Day 1-3

- Roosters court hens, leading to fertilization.
- Hens lay eggs, marking the beginning of the incubation process.

## The Incubation Chamber

### Day 1-7

The incubation process begins with carefully placing fertilized eggs in an incubator. The eggs must be positioned with the pointed end slightly lower to facilitate proper embryonic development.

- Gather eggs, ensuring cleanliness.
- Place eggs in the incubator with proper orientation.

### Day 7-14

- Embryo development begins.
- Initial candling to observe embryonic growth.

## Mid-Incubation

### Day 14-18

- Continued embryo development.
- Regular candling to track progress.

### Day 18-19

- Stop turning eggs.
- Increase humidity for hatching readiness.

## Hatching

### Day 19-21

- **Pipping**: This is the process where the chick starts to break through the eggshell using its egg tooth.
- **Hatching**: The final milestone is the actual hatching of the chicks. This process can take anywhere from a few hours to a day. Chicks use their egg tooth to make a small hole (pipping) and gradually work their way out of the shell.

### Day 21-22

- Transfer chicks to the brooder.
- Initial feedings and health checks.

# The Incubation Process

Whether you're a novice or a seasoned enthusiast, this step-by-step guide will lead you through setting up your incubator, regulating temperature and humidity, and closely monitoring the development of embryos for a successful hatching experience.

## Step 1: Setting Up the Incubator

### Choose the Right Incubator

Begin by selecting an incubator that aligns with your specific requirements. Consider factors such as egg capacity, automatic turning features, and temperature control capabilities.

#### Placement Matters

Make sure that the incubator is positioned in a stable environment, away from direct sunlight and drafts. Consistent temperature regulation is crucial for the success of the incubation process.

#### Sanitize and Prepare

Thoroughly clean the incubator, including trays and any accessories, to eliminate potential contaminants. Sterilize the incubator with a mild disinfectant to establish a hygienic environment.

#### Calibrate the Incubator

Calibrate the incubator to guarantee accurate temperature readings. Use a reliable thermometer to cross-verify the incubator's temperature settings, ensuring precision.

## Step 2: Temperature and Humidity Regulation

### Set the Initial Temperature

Eggs generally require an initial temperature of approximately 99.5°F (37.5°C). Adjust the incubator's thermostat to achieve and maintain this temperature. These conditions simulate the natural environment necessary for embryo development. Keep a close eye on the temperature by checking it regularly. Any fluctuations can significantly impact embryo development. Adjust promptly to maintain stability.

#### Humidity Control

Maintain humidity levels within the recommended range for your specific eggs. Typically, a 40-50% relative humidity is suitable for the first

18 days, increasing to 65-75% during the lockdown period.

### Water Management

Use a hygrometer to accurately measure humidity. Adjust it by adding water to the incubator trays, considering a larger water surface area to increase humidity.

# Step 3: Turning Eggs and Lockdown

Regularly turning eggs is critical to prevent the embryo from sticking to the shell. Birds instinctively do this in nature, but this process is replicated mechanically or manually in an incubator.

### Automatic Turners

If your incubator has an automatic turner, make sure it is activated. Turning the eggs at regular intervals is essential for embryo development. For manual turning, do this at least three times a day.

### Lockdown Preparation

On day 18, stop turning the eggs and prepare for lockdown. Increase humidity by adding more water to the trays. Lockdown simulates the natural nest environment, creating ideal conditions for hatching.

# Step 4: Monitoring Embryo Development

### Candling

Around day seven and day 14, start candling to assess signs of development. Look for veins, embryo movement, and healthy growth. Remove any clear or non-viable eggs to maintain optimal conditions.

### Record Keeping

Maintain a comprehensive log of vital information, including incubator settings, candling observations, and any adjustments made. Meticulous record-keeping helps with troubleshooting and serves as a valuable reference for future incubations.

You establish an optimal environment for successful incubation by diligently following these detailed steps. Remember, each egg holds the promise of life, and your careful attention guarantees a seamless journey from incubation to the joyous moment of hatching.

### Practicing Patience

It's the cornerstone of a breeder's journey. The incubation process unfolds gradually, requiring steadfast patience. This process demands waiting, and waiting demands patience. It's a delicate dance where time plays a crucial role in the development of life within the eggs. Patience allows nature to unfurl at its own pace.

Patience in observation aids in detecting early signs of potential issues. Recognizing irregularities allows for timely adjustments, fostering a proactive approach to incubation management.

### Post-Hatching Care

Welcoming a new batch of chicks into the world is a joyous occasion, but it comes with the responsibility to provide impeccable care during the critical first days post-hatch. This section will delve into chick care, brooding, and early nutrition to ensure a healthy and thriving start for your newfound feathered friends.

# Chick Care

### Drying Off

Welcoming chicks into the world involves allowing them to undergo a natural process of drying off after hatching. This initial step is crucial in ensuring the health and well-being of the newly hatched chicks.

### Natural Drying Process

Chicks emerge from their eggs wet. This moisture is a result of the hatching process and the remnants of the eggshell's contents. The chicks, however, possess a natural instinct to commence the drying process almost immediately after hatching.

Allowing chicks to dry off naturally is vital. The dampness on their bodies serves a purpose in the wild, where it helps insulate the chicks during the hatching process. This down, once dried, contributes to the chick's ability to regulate its body temperature.

During the initial moments post-hatch, resist the urge to intervene. Observing the chicks as they fluff their feathers and dry naturally provides valuable insights into their vitality. Active, healthy chicks exhibit vigorous movements to shed excess moisture.

# Implementing Biosecurity Measures

### Isolation and Quarantine

Establish a dedicated area for the brooder that is physically separate from other poultry or animals. This minimizes the risk of potential disease transmission between different groups of birds.

### Restricted Access

Limit access to the brooder area strictly to essential personnel. Enforce stringent hygiene protocols, including the use of dedicated clothing and footwear when entering the space, to prevent the introduction of contaminants.

### Hand Hygiene

Enforce thorough hand hygiene practices for anyone handling chicks. Provide easily accessible handwashing stations equipped with soap and water or hand sanitizer near the brooder area to reduce the risk of disease spread.

### Footwear Sanitization

Set up footbaths (or foot mats containing disinfectant) solutions at the entrance of the brooder area. This measure ensures that footwear, a potential carrier of pathogens, is disinfected before entering the space.

### Clean and Disinfect Equipment

Regularly clean and disinfect all equipment used in the brooder, including feeders, waterers, and any other tools. Use effective disinfectants recommended for poultry facilities to eliminate potential disease vectors.

### Avoiding Interference

While assisting in the drying process might be tempting, interference is generally unnecessary. The warmth of the incubator or brooder gradually provides the ideal environment for the chicks to dry off without external assistance.

### Separating Weak Chicks

As part of the immediate care routine, assessing each chick for signs of weakness or lethargy is essential. If identified, weak chicks should be gently separated for special attention to give them the care they need to thrive.

### Prevent Overcrowding

Overcrowding can lead to stress, injuries, and competition for resources. Ensure that the brooder space allows each chick sufficient room to move, eat, and drink comfortably.

Biosecurity is crucial to prevent the spread of diseases. Practicing good hygiene, including regular cleaning of the brooder, disinfecting equipment, and washing hands before handling chicks, contributes to maintaining a healthy environment.

### Gradual Introduction to Solid Food

Around the second or third day, chicks can be introduced to solid food in addition to the starter feed. This broader diet stimulates their natural foraging instincts.

### Adjust Brooder Conditions Gradually

As the chicks grow, they gradually adjust the brooder conditions to mimic the natural environment. Lowering the temperature and providing opportunities for exploration and socialization contribute to their overall well-being.

### Transferring to Brooder

Once the chicks are visibly dry and active, it's time to transfer them to the brooder. The brooder replicates the warmth and security of a natural nesting environment, creating a conducive space for the chicks' further development.

### Brooding Essentials

Creating the right environment for newly hatched chicks is crucial for their health, growth, and overall well-being. The brooding essentials encompass a range of factors that contribute to a comfortable and secure space.

### Appropriate Temperature

Maintaining the right temperature within the brooder is paramount for the chicks' survival. During the first week, aim for a temperature of around 95°F (35°C) and gradually decrease it by 5°F (2.8°C) each week until the chicks feather out. Use a reliable thermometer placed at the chick level for accurate readings.

### Bedding Material

Choose a suitable bedding material for the brooder. Pine shavings are a popular choice, providing a non-slippery surface for chicks to move around. The bedding maintains cleanliness and provides insulation against temperature fluctuations.

### Ample Space

Make sure that the brooder offers sufficient space for the chicks to move freely. Overcrowding can lead to stress and potential health issues. Adequate space also prevents competition for resources and encourages natural behaviors.

### Access to Feed and Water

Place chick feed in shallow containers to facilitate easy access. Fresh, clean water should be available at all times. Dip each chick's beak in the water upon introduction to help them locate the water source. Adequate feeder and waterer space prevents crowding and ensures all chicks have access.

### Lighting Conditions

Maintain appropriate lighting conditions in the brooder. Provide a balance between light and dark periods, allowing chicks to rest. Adequate lighting supports healthy circadian rhythms and helps chicks establish a regular feeding and resting routine.

### Ventilation

Ensure proper ventilation in the brooder to prevent ammonia buildup and maintain air quality. Drafts, however, should be avoided, as they can lead to chilling. Strike a balance between fresh air circulation and maintaining a warm environment.

### Brooder Placement

Choose a strategic location for the brooder. It should be situated away from drafts, direct sunlight, and areas with extreme temperature fluctuations. Placing the brooder in a quiet and low-traffic area helps reduce stress for the chicks.

### Monitoring Equipment

Use monitoring equipment, like a thermometer and hygrometer, to regularly check the temperature and humidity levels. These tools assist in making necessary adjustments to create an optimal environment.

### Supplemental Heat Sources

Depending on the brooding setup, supplemental heat sources like heat lamps or radiant heaters may be required. Position these sources to create a temperature gradient within the brooder, allowing chicks to choose their preferred comfort zone.

Creating a comfortable space within the brooder involves meticulously considering temperature, space, cleanliness, and environmental factors. Addressing these brooding essentials establishes the foundation for a healthy and thriving flock as the chicks grow and develop.

# Early Nutrition

The early stages of a chick's life are critical for establishing a foundation of health and vitality. Early nutrition plays a pivotal role in supporting their growth and development. The following section covers the various aspects of providing optimal nutrition to ensure a strong start for your chicks.

### Selecting the Right Feed

Choosing a high-quality chick starter feed is fundamental to meeting the nutritional needs of growing chicks. Look for a feed with around 18-20% protein content, designed specifically for the early stages of poultry development. The balanced formulation should include essential vitamins and minerals for bone, muscle, and organ development.

### Supplementation

Consider supplementing the chicks' diet with a vitamin-electrolyte supplement in their water during the first few days. This supplementation supports their immune system, helps counteract any stress during the transition, and ensures they receive essential nutrients for optimal health.

### Feeder Accessibility

The feed should be easily accessible in shallow containers within the brooder. Chicks should be able to reach the feed to encourage consistent and adequate consumption. Positioning the feeders at an appropriate height facilitates easy access for all chicks.

### Water Accessibility

Provide fresh, clean water at all times. Chicks need to stay hydrated, particularly during their early days. Dip each chick's beak in the water upon introduction to familiarize them with its location. Hydration is crucial for digestion, nutrient absorption, and overall well-being.

### Monitoring Feed Consumption

Regularly monitor the chicks' feed consumption. Healthy chicks will exhibit a consistent appetite. Adjust feeding amounts if needed, considering environmental conditions and individual chick requirements. All chicks should have equal access to feed.

### Brooder Temperature and Nutrition

The brooder's temperature influences the chicks' metabolic rate and, consequently, their nutritional requirements. Adjust the feed and water supply based on temperature changes, ensuring the chicks receive adequate nutrition to support their growth and maintain body temperature.

### Health Monitoring

Nutrition is closely linked to overall health. Monitor the chicks for malnutrition or deficiencies, such as lethargy, stunted growth, or abnormal feather development. Address any nutritional concerns promptly. Furthermore, maintain a detailed record of the chicks' feeding patterns and any observed changes in behavior or health. This record is valuable for adjusting their diet as they progress through different developmental stages.

### Transition to Grower Feed

As the chicks mature, transition them to a grower feed with a slightly lower protein content. This gradual shift aligns with their changing nutritional requirements and supports the development of feathers and skeletal structure.

# Performing Health Checks

Maintaining the health of your chicks is a continuous process that involves thorough health checks and keen observation. Regular assessments ensure that any potential issues are identified and addressed promptly, contributing to the overall well-being of your flock.

### Daily Health Assessments

Conduct daily health assessments of each chick. This allows you to identify any subtle changes in behavior, appearance, or activity levels. Healthy chicks exhibit alertness, curiosity, and responsive behavior.

### Physical Appearance

Examine the chicks for any abnormalities in their physical appearance. Check for clear eyes, well-groomed feathers, and clean vents. Abnormalities like disheveled feathers, discharge from the eyes or nostrils, or changes in posture can indicate potential health issues.

### Active Behavior

Monitor the chicks for active and engaged behavior. Lively chicks exploring their surroundings, pecking, and interacting with their environment are signs of good health. Lethargy, excessive sleepiness, or reluctance to move may indicate underlying problems.

## Feeding Behavior

Observe the chicks during feeding times. A healthy appetite is a positive sign. Any changes in feeding behavior, such as a sudden decrease in consumption or increased aggression during feeding, should be noted.

## Social Interaction

Chickens are social animals, and healthy chicks engage in social interactions.
*https://unsplash.com/photos/white-and-pink-rabbit-plush-toy-on-yellow-plastic-basin-XOGg38VufZs*

Chickens are social animals, and healthy chicks engage in social interactions. Observe their behavior with each other, ensuring that all chicks are integrated into the flock. Isolation or aggressive pecking may signal social issues or potential health concerns.

## Respiratory Health

Monitor respiratory health by listening for normal breathing sounds. Respiratory distress, audible wheezing, or labored breathing can be indicators of respiratory infections. Inspect the nares (nostrils) for any signs of discharge.

## Vent Check

Regularly check the vents of the chicks for cleanliness. This is where eggs are laid. A clean vent indicates proper digestive health. Any signs of diarrhea or abnormalities in fecal consistency should be addressed straight away.

## Weight Monitoring

Implement periodic weight monitoring. Gradual weight gain is a positive sign of healthy development. Sudden weight loss or fluctuations may signal underlying issues and should be investigated.

## Record Keeping

Maintain a detailed record of health observations, including any abnormalities, interventions, and outcomes. This record becomes a valuable resource for identifying patterns, tracking progress, and informing future care strategies.

## Prompt Intervention

If any health concerns are identified during checks, intervene promptly. Isolate affected chicks, if necessary, consult with a veterinarian, and implement appropriate measures to address the issue.

## Environmental Factors

Consider environmental factors that may impact health, such as changes in temperature, humidity, or ventilation. Ensure that the brooder environment remains conducive to optimal health.

You establish a proactive approach to their well-being by consistently conducting health checks and keenly observing your chicks. Early detection of potential issues allows for timely intervention, ensuring a healthier and more robust flock as your chicks progress through their developmental stages.

# Chapter 7: The "Pecking Order": Social Dynamics

At first glance, it may seem like there is no social structure among farm birds. Anyone who has not observed chickens, ducks, or turkeys for an extended time can be forgiven for making this uninformed assumption. To successfully raise poultry, you need to be familiar with how the birds you choose interact socially so you can manage your flock according to their nature. Birds do not have the mental complexity that people do, so you must get onto their level of thinking to understand them. Moreover, seeing how their communication methods are vastly different from those of people, you must learn their language.

Poultry birds mostly arrange their groups in a hierarchical social structure known as a pecking order.

Poultry birds mostly arrange their groups in a hierarchical social structure known as a pecking order. There may be slight delineations between species, but the idea remains relatively the same. When you understand the social dynamics of your flock, you can create an environment that minimizes injury and facilitates reproduction. Birds can be aggressive, but in the same vein, they have a collective and cooperative society.

The environment will affect how your birds behave. Competition for food and mates can become a problem if it is not managed. For example, in overcrowded conditions, some chickens starve to death because the fights are so brutal. Weaker birds avoid fighting, so they never get to eat. Many poultry species live in groups, so they can be tribal. Understanding their vocalizations and body language will allow you to respond to various behaviors.

You can become a poultry mind reader by noticing a few behavioral cues. Birds do not express their emotions and concerns like people do, nor do they resolve their conflicts in the same way. You need to be a mediating force to direct the outcome you desire in your flock. Your oversight and knowledge basically make you the president of your mini-bird nation. Great governance of your flock requires you to tap into the variety of social expressions it exhibits.

## Origins of Order

Evolution by natural selection is the foundation of all the behavior of living organisms. Survival of the fittest is often misinterpreted to mean that might is right or that the strongest animals rise to the top. This is not necessarily the case. As much as huge elephants are evolutionarily successful, tiny butterflies were also chosen by nature. Therefore, survival of the fittest means that nature will keep traits most suited to environmental conditions. Evolutionarily, birds are some of the oldest species on the planet, and there's even evidence they're related to dinosaurs. However, you can see some traces of their ancestry when you look at ostriches or emus, which can be terrifying if you are not accustomed to their intimidating appearances.

All adaptations are based on the availability of resources and the drive to reproduce. The hierarchical structure of fowl society has been instilled over millions of years of evolution. Although some traits of many farmed species have been artificially bred into existence by humans, the ways poultry structure their social groups predate human intervention. If you look at wild ducks or turkeys, they have the same types of societal organization as their domesticated cousins. All behaviors evolve in an environmental context. The societies that various poultry birds have developed are what have allowed them to remain on the planet for so long. Making the connection between why behaviors develop in particular environments and why they are evolutionarily beneficial will grant you the keys to understanding their psychology. Some of the natural behaviors that these birds display could be in opposition to the type of raising operation you are establishing. To encourage the behaviors you want, you must manipulate their environment. Therefore, you need to guide them toward the behaviors you would like to see with the help of psychology and evolutionary biology by making conscious changes so that your birds adopt favorable expressions.

Domestic ducks most likely descend from two duck species, namely the wild mallard and the Chinese spot-billed duck. Selective breeding and differing environments also play a role in shifting the social behavior of fowl species. Certain behaviors are kept from their evolutionary past. For example, many duck species pair bond and have courting displays for mating. Typically, the male of the species will make elaborate movements to attract a female. The competition amongst males will be fierce, with many suitors fighting for the opportunity to show off their skills. Furthermore, the mating seasons for some bird species come along once a year for a short period of time, so they are keenly aware that they have little time to woo a partner.

It is believed that this tough competition is a result of the female population being lower than the males. This is because females, in addition to being physically weaker, also perform tasks that put them in increased danger, like nesting. Therefore, not every male will get a mate, and the female has to choose wisely whose genes she wants to pass on. The elaborate courtship rituals allow the female to make an informed choice by examining the physicality of her potential partners.

There is power in numbers. Many fowl species have evolved social cohesion because they can respond to threats better when sticking together. Groups are better able to ward off predators with warning systems, and they can forage better because there are more ways to look out for food. Chicken societies are remarkably close to humans. They have surprisingly complex relationships that have evolved over millions of years. Humans can process about 150 social relations, while chickens can process about 30. The stereotype of a "bird brain" being stupid is far from accurate. Chickens know exactly where they sit on their social ladder. Since chickens can only remember about 30 relationships, it becomes tougher to introduce new birds into a large group.

Fowl hierarchies may seem violent at first glance, but the social order that these birds develop is an evolutionary trait that emerged to reduce fights. If a duck knows where it stands in the social order, it will not typically fight members higher up in the ranks. This creates a solid society with reduced instability. Natural selection chose the social structure of fowl because it protects them from predators, allows them to get food, and reduces fights within a flock.

In a social order, there must be ways to communicate. If not, the structure will quickly fall apart. Fowls have developed vocalizations and body language to communicate their needs and disagreements. You need to be familiar with these sounds and movements to maintain the well-being of your flock. Observation is your main tool because it will inform any other actions that you take concerning your flock.

The environments that birds live in profoundly impact their behavior, showing evolutionary development in real time. For example, city ducks have a louder quack than those in rural areas because the noise levels are higher in densely populated and industrialized regions. Similar to humans, there are cultural differences between birds of the same species based on where they are from. This adaptation shows how powerful human interference can be. The environment you build for your animals will change how they interact, so you must be keenly aware of how your actions impact your flock. If you are not careful about how you engage with your birds, any small change you make could have a huge impact. To get into a bird's mind, use empathy instead of visual cues.

Many different kinds of fowl show deep family connections that have evolved for the purposes of safety and resource acquisition. In turkey populations, after about six months, the males will form sibling groups that typically last a lifetime. Amongst swans and ducks, pairs mate for life, with some widows and widowers refusing to mate with a new partner even after the death of their partner. Much like human families act as a support to help people thrive and survive, animals like ducks, turkeys, and swans employ the same strategy.

Sticking together, minimizing competition, collectively searching for food, and having access to mates are the underpinnings of most evolutionary fowl behavior. Understanding what your birds are doing through these lenses will help your flock produce the outcomes you desire. You are meant to hack the adaptations of your birds to direct them toward your goals. You must understand how they evolved to provide them with adequate care that satisfies all of their needs. When you begin poultry farming, you are adopted as an honorary member of the flock that has the most responsibilities.

## Signs and Signals

Just like humans have various signs and signals they use to communicate their state of being, so do fowls. Someone might start talking louder and getting redder if they are angry, or they may laugh out loud when they are happy. A woman might give a man a look hinting she is interested, and he may reply with a winning smile to show his interest. All these social dynamics frame the way humans relate to one another. There are many overlaps in the fowl kingdom. Although the males do not have any teeth to flash a movie star smile, and some species don't turn red when angry, they have their unique body language and vocalizations to communicate their needs and displeasures. The environment they are kept in will influence their actions, and their behavior can vary depending on what you do as a farmer.

Sally had started a permaculture homestead where she grew a variety of produce and kept many different kinds of animals. She decided to breed ducks to sell them to contribute to the maintenance of her farm. She noticed that when she introduced new ducks into her flock, they were attacked and prevented from feeding. That almost always led her to separate them. After learning a bit more about the social dynamics of ducks, she devised a new method to introduce new members of the flock. Sally constructed a cage adjacent to where her other ducks were kept. She would let them interact through the mesh fence. By gradually introducing new ducks, she was able to manage the violent aggression that her birds showed.

Ducks hiss and spread their wings when they are angry. This is done to intimidate threats and make themselves look bigger. When there are too many males in a flock, this behavior becomes common, especially if there is not a lot of space. Duck fights increase during mating season because males are hardwired to compete for mates. Even on a farm where females outnumber males, they may still fight during the mating season.

There are many interesting ways different kinds of fowl species express themselves. Turkeys change color according to their emotional state. The featherless turkey head will be lighter shades when they are calm but will transform into a deep red if they are angry or stressed. The snood, which is that little bit of wrinkly, dangling flesh near the turkey's beak, works in combination with its head color changing. Red does not always equal aggression. The snood will contract if a turkey is scared and about to fly away. For an aggressive or relaxed turkey, the snood will hang loosely. An angry one might charge to warn or intimidate you. This behavior must be monitored because domestic turkeys have a greater chance of fatally injuring one another than their wild counterparts because they live in such proximity to one another.

Identifying the roles your birds play in their social order is a big part of being able to manage them. If you can identify those at the top of the hierarchy, you know the ones that you need your new members to impress. Sounds and body language can help you find the alpha out of the bunch. If you look at turkeys, for example, the classic gobble noise you hear coming from them is either to attract females or to assert dominance. If you hear a few members of your flock gobbling more than others, they are probably the leaders. They are the ones that need the most convincing when introducing new birds. Turkeys are especially hostile to outsiders because they rely on their group for survival. They will need some convincing for new members to enter.

Many other vocalizations will tell you the mood your turkeys are in. You need to know what every sound means because how your turkeys are doing will determine the peacefulness of your flock. When turkeys are content, they cluck and purr. When you hear these noises, know that your flock is in a great position socially. Mothers usually let out loud and continuous yelps to gather their young. Even though this sound pierces your ears, there is no problem that needs addressing at that moment.

With chickens, although roosters are persistently competing for the top position, there are also social classes among hens as well. The head hen is the one that eats first. She will get her choice of the best nesting position. The rooster hierarchy is linked but separated from the hens. If a rooster chooses to interfere with the hierarchy that the hens have built, they will sometimes gang up on him to attack the one in charge. The hens will rotate guard duty to look out for predators, but the alpha hen does most of the work. When there is danger approaching, the hen on the lookout will let out an eardrum-rattling screech to warn the others. The pecking order of hens may be on the verge of transition when you see challenges arise. The hens competing for the number one spot will stare one another down and puff out their neck feathers before fighting. These challenges could happen repeatedly until either one of the competitors gives up. If you cannot risk your birds getting injured, it may be advisable to separate them at times like this. Alpha hens will emerge even if there are no roosters in your flock.

# Managing Disruptions

There are four major causes of conflict among fowl species. Fowls like having a lot of space. When you put them in cramped conditions, it increases their stress, which results in more fighting. Mating is another cause for conflict, so you need to maintain your male-to-female ratio at an acceptable level. Food resources could also be a cause for conflict. Fighting over food goes hand in hand with being in cramped spaces, which is why battery-caged chicken farmers remove the beaks of their flock to reduce damage. Lastly, since many fowl species form deep social bonds, they may also fight if new birds are introduced in a type of tribal gang violence. Much like pack or herd animals, poultry birds are territorial because of the competition for resources. You need to get your flock to understand that the newest member is part of the group.

When you put them in cramped conditions, it increases their stress, which results in more fighting.

Poultry is similar to humans when it comes to how adverse conditions stoke the flames of antisocial behavior. To keep your flock well-behaved, make sure they are well-fed, have ample space to explore and perch, as well as a good mixture of males and females. That does not mean there will never be any hiccups. Fowls have their societal perception, so battles will emerge for hierarchical positioning. You cannot completely eradicate fighting, but you can minimize it. A calm, spacious area reduces the short-tempered birds' irritability.

Farm birds do not reserve their aggression for each other. When an alpha rooster emerges, you may find that they start attacking you. Chevanni started a backyard chicken coop for egg production and to add to the overall feel of his home. One of the roosters, named Frango, which means chicken in Portuguese, became overly aggressive. He was the only chicken with a name because he had the most personality. Frango would not let anybody walk past from a distance closer than about four feet. It'd flap its wings and lunge at you, pecking any bit of exposed skin. It terrified people, although it was not able to cause much harm. It became unpleasant because whenever children visited, they would have to watch out for Frango. Many people made sure they took the long way around the house just to avoid it.

In cases like this, there are some steps you can take to address the undesirable behavior. Ignoring the attacks will not make them go away. The longer you wait, the more the behavior will become ingrained. Remember that a rooster does not hate people. It sees you as a threat, so all it is doing is protecting the hens. Some people use water spray bottles to keep them at bay. Spraying a rooster with water is uncomfortable but does not hurt the animal. Your best option in this case, if you are brave enough, is flipping your rooster. When it starts acting in violent ways, grab it, flip it upside down, and hold it close to your body until it calms down. This would need to be repeated regularly until it begins adjusting its behavior.

Ducks can be notoriously territorial. Unlike roosters, their attacks are extremely painful and will leave you with giant bruises. There are several ways to get aggressive ducks under control. The first technique you could try is to eliminate hand feeding. Hand feeding can cause aggression amongst your animals because hierarchies are established when some animals get more feed than others. Instead of hand feeding, scatter the food and allow them to forage. The feed you choose could also impact your animal's temperament. For ducks, choose food that contains more greens and that is protein-rich. An abundance of energy could be the culprit for their unpredictable behavior. You can use toys or take them for a swim to use up some of their excess energy. Lastly, you can pin the duck down on their back. This takes away their primary defenses, their beaks, and wings. It also asserts your dominance as their leader, but you must be careful because there is still a chance of getting injured in the process.

Be mindful of how your actions are perceived by your animals. You may assume that you are behaving appropriately, but birds do not interpret actions the same way as humans do. You may think you are spoiling your ducks by giving them treats, but this teaches them to expect food from humans, and, in some cases, this could turn ugly. You need to be hyper-aware of the psychology of your birds and frame all your actions according to what they understand and how you would like your coop to be run.

# Chapter 8: Fowl Play: Dealing with Predators

Imagine putting in all the effort to understand what goes into choosing the right birds, taking all the necessary health precautions, fully grasping the dynamics of breeding, and understanding their social interactions just for a sneaky devil to munch on your entire flock. Waking up to dead birds is both traumatizing and heartbreaking. Dealing with predators can become a constant mission, but with hard work and the right information, you can manage to keep them away.

Combatting predators is all about how you house your birds. However, this task can become complicated due to the lack of a one-size-fits-all solution. Preparing your coop for fox attacks and leaving it vulnerable to snakes will not work. You need to be able to identify predators in your area and equip your enclosures to respond to all possible challenges. From fencing and housing to the identification of predators and adjusting to the local environment, the following chapter will assist you in responding to all predator threats.

As much as it can be devastating for your birds to be harmed, it does not justify acting violently against predators, especially if they are federally protected like owls and hawks. Harming protected animals carries harsh legal repercussions. Protecting your birds should be humane and be carried out with respect for the well-being of the predators. In some cases, you can contact government bodies to remove the predators.

Exploring your options may come with a lot of mistakes along the way. There is no exact science to predator prevention. What you have at your exposal is not the same as what the next person has. Conducting a detailed analysis and researching all the variables about your birds and their predators is the foundation on which you should start building. Once your coop and fencing are up, predators may find some weak spots. You will use this to conduct reconnaissance about the predator's behavior and make changes according to the gaps. As the seasons change, this battle will be a constant one. When your structures deteriorate, be ready to continuously observe and respond. The cat-and-mouse game you play with predators may be unending, but once your main structure is in place, you will only need to make small repairs and changes.

## Predator Profiles

Whether you are keeping your birds in a major city or out in the most isolated woods, predators are always a major threat. Domesticated dogs and cats can be just as dangerous as foxes or coyotes. Other unexpected visitors might show up – like raccoons or rats looking to nibble on chicks or have an egg as a midnight snack. Different regions have varying predators, so it helps to know which animals are common in your area so that you can adjust your preparations accordingly. If your flock has already been attacked, there are some steps you can take to determine what the threat is. How your animals are killed (and which tracks or droppings are left behind) are all clues to point you in the direction of the right culprit.

Coyotes are common re-offenders when it comes to taking out poultry.
https://www.pexels.com/photo/coyote-lying-on-grass-10226903/

Coyotes are common re-offenders when it comes to taking out poultry. They easily sneak past defenses and are often cunning enough not to get caught. They are creative and find unusual ways to get into your enclosures. If you hear regular howling in your area, you may have a problem with coyotes. Although the mere presence of scat is not an indicator that it came from a predator, it can help to identify the droppings. Coyotes, for example, use droppings to communicate, so those will be easy to spot. It often contains hair and bones. They have similar tracks to dogs, except their prints are slimmer, streamlined, and more oval. Their tendency to find unexpected points of entry means that following their tracks could help you determine where they broke in. You will probably not find many parts of your bird because coyotes kill and carry away the animal, so blood and feathers will be all that's left.

Foxes are a lot like coyotes in their slyness and appearance.
https://www.pexels.com/photo/brown-and-white-fox-on-green-grass-3739926/

Foxes are a lot like coyotes in their slyness and appearance. Coyotes have brown coats, while foxes have red and gray coats. Foxes are found in many states around the US and even in Canada. They live in holes they dig into the ground near trees or walls. If you find these dens on or near your property, you are most definitely dealing with foxes. Wildlife organizations are often willing to relocate them if you find any on your property. This is done to stop farmers from killing these animals so they can thrive in the wild.

**Rats are not picky eaters, so they enjoy both chicks and eggs.**
*https://www.pexels.com/photo/closeup-photo-of-tan-rat-1010267/*

One unexpected predator is rats. They cannot attack fully grown birds, but you may find some bites on their legs. Rats are not picky eaters, so they enjoy both chicks and eggs. Keeping them out can be extremely tough, so many farmers resort to poisoning. You will find the small droppings along the corners of your coop, and you may also discover parts of chicks stuck in holes that the rats burrowed in or squeezed through.

Weasels, minks, and skunks are all small predators that, like rats, are difficult to keep out of your coop. To keep them out, you must be thorough with your construction because there cannot be gaps bigger than about half an inch. Weasels can be particularly brutal because they not only kill for prey but also take enjoyment in hunting. If you find a decapitated chicken, there is likely a weasel in the picture. Weasels can take out large parts of your flock at once because of their capacity to kill for fun. If you do not discover them in the act, you'll enter your coop to discover massive destruction with bites on your birds' necks and backs. Skunks and weasels also leave behind a musky smell, so a potent fragrance is a giveaway of their presence.

Raccoons have hand-like paws, so they can open simple locks, and they find crafty ways to break into your coop.

https://www.pexels.com/photo/close-up-photo-of-raccoons-14050298/

Opossums and raccoons are in trouble in cities and rural areas alike. You do not have to worry that much about opossums because they are lazy hunters and will only kill sick birds. As long as you make it difficult for them to enter, you should be okay. The main problem with opossums is not their killing capabilities but the diseases they carry. Raccoons, on the other hand, are a nuisance. They have hand-like paws so they can open simple locks, and they find crafty ways to break into your coop. If there are raccoons around, your birds need to be well-secured. They are destructive and will leave a trail of half-eaten bodies lying around. The clean-up after a raccoon attack can be extremely nasty. Leaving animals headless and limbless is their calling card.

Domestic pets like cats and dogs can be massive problems, too. Make sure that your animals are trained and accustomed to the birds you have on your land. Pets are usually fed by their owners, so these animals do not kill birds for food but rather a predatory instinct. A good sign that cats or dogs are the culprits is that the birds will be dead but not eaten. Pets usually kill for sport instead of food. Your pets can be trained, but sometimes your neighbor's animals get into your yard, so you need a good relationship with the people who live around you so you can work together to protect your flock.

**Bobcats are small but deadly.**
*https://www.pexels.com/photo/animal-animal-photography-big-big-cat-209032/*

Bobcats terrorize many parts of rural and urban North America. These cats are small but deadly. They are stealthy hunters, so it is unlikely that you will spot one on your property unless you have cameras. They almost always aim for the head. If you find your bird headless, a bobcat might be the one to blame. Their droppings contain fragments of vegetation and look similar to those of a domesticated house cat. Their prints resemble house cats as well, but are bigger. If you smell cat urine, there is a chance that it belongs to a bobcat.

Depending on where you live, you will most probably not be defending your animals against one type of predator. A holistic approach that caters to several variables is the best route to take. The predators on your land may change according to season, so stay prepared for all possibilities. Whether the predators are punching, scurrying, flying, or slithering, you must have an answer to the attack techniques. Using paws, fecal matter, killing methods, and smells, you can see exactly what you are dealing with so that you can act aligned with what you have discovered. Going in equipped with a bunch of signs to look for puts you ahead of the game so that you can react quickly.

## Fortifying the Flock

In commercial farms, predators are not much of an issue because birds are typically kept inside buildings until they are mature enough for slaughter. However, with smaller homesteads, organic farms, and backyard operations, predator attacks are likely. When you construct an enclosure for your animals, there are several factors you need to consider, like the number of birds you have, the predators and risks you have in your area, and the costs and supplies you have available. Building a coop is a constant process of trial and error to find what works best for your unique needs. Constant adjustments must be made until you find what is functional.

Many organic farmers are set in their old ways of dealing with predators. Killing or poisoning animals are not ideal options for protecting your birds. The local ecosystem is sensitive, so you should always strive to make ethical and humane decisions. Some animals are protected by law, but this does not stop farmers from shooting and burying animals on their property. This is by no means an ethical approach, especially if you are embracing organic farming to protect the environment and ethically raise livestock. A prime example of an organic farmer who embodies ethical agriculture is Will Harris, who runs the family farm White Oak Pastures in Georgia.

Harris had a problem with bald eagles making easy pickings of his flock. The farmer admired the birds and lived alongside them. However, he began reconsidering his pacifist attitude when the birds began attacking his turkeys in addition to his chickens. He looks at the losses as a sacrifice or tithe to nature. He believes in permaculture organic farming. Instead of killing the birds like many farmers do, Harris contacted the Georgia Department of Natural Resources or DNR. There is not much that the department could do for the overgrown eagle population, so Harris still lives with the birds taking on the losses. He believes that if all the farmers in the area used organic farming methods, the eagles would naturally spread and scatter, but he admits that this small-scale farming revolution is unlikely to happen. At the last count, 75 eagles were living on and around the property. These huge numbers of eagles killed thousands of his birds.

Predator-friendly farming, like Will Harris adopted, is an option, but not everyone has a large enough farm or the resources to take such losses. One of the first options you can explore to protect your animals is constructing floorless grazing coops. These will stand about two to three feet high, depending on the species you are farming. The width and length of the coop will depend on how many birds you have. These coops protect your animals from aerial attacks during the day.

Therefore, they are handy for birds of prey that hunt during sunlight hours, like eagles or hawks. Some birds, like owls, hunt at night. To prevent these attacks, you should build a safe, roofed structure to put your livestock into at night after they are done feeding. Make use of orange netting because it distracts the vision of birds like hawks and owls.

Motion-sensing lights are a great deterrent for nocturnal animals. These hunters usually have brilliant eyesight in the dark, but this could make them sensitive to extreme changes in light. The bright and instant flash that comes from motion sensors can scare these predators, keeping them away from your precious livestock. Moreover, the increased visibility on your land can help you spot predators better in the dark so you can know exactly which animals you are dealing with and craft your prevention methods specifically for them.

An age-old method of pest control is the use of guard animals. Domestic cats are great for keeping rats and even snakes away from your birds, while dogs can deal with bigger predators like coyotes or foxes. If you use guard animals, they need to be well-trained and used to living with poultry because sometimes they can be problems themselves. Cats can be dangerous for local bird populations, so they aren't always a great choice for sustainability, but they are effective for small predators. The downside of using guard animals is that they kill the predators, which is not the most humane way to get rid of them.

Sometimes, you need to think outside of the box. The box, in this case, creates a solid, unbreakable coop. You may find yourself continuously having to restructure your pens because different predators keep finding their way in, but you must expand your gaze outwards. For example, birds of prey could be hanging around your property because it is comfortable and attractive to them. Removing perches taller than 100 yards will encourage the squatters to leave. You may need to cut down some trees on your property to get rid of pesky flying predators.

With mesh fencing, wood, metals, and some basic building expertise, you can construct coops that will keep the majority of predators out. Unlike commercial farms that have protected concrete buildings with fowl cramped in battery cages, your free-range setup is not as secure. Your vigilance and ingenuity are your biggest weapons against predator encroachment. Use what you have wisely, and cater your protection plans to the psychology of the species threatening your population.

# When Breaches Happen

You may think that you have a solid, foolproof plan to protect your birds, but small damages to your enclosures or simple oversights can result in predators gaining entry to your coop. You need to respond quickly when this happens because you know that predators have an open pathway to an all-you-can-eat buffet. Keep some repair materials around at all times, like metals, mesh fencing, wood, zinc, nails, glue, and construction tools like hammers, saws, and drills. You can quickly put together a makeshift patch until you come up with a better solution. These repair patches could be the difference between losing your entire flock or losing just a few birds and eggs.

Joyce Bupp struggled with predators killing her chickens. At this point, her birds produced very few eggs, and they were more like pets. Losing them affected her deeply. She struggled to know exactly which animals were eating her pets because there were several different predators on her farm. Eventually, she discovered a small hole through which a raccoon was entering under the cover of night. They trapped the omnivorous culprit using sweet corn as bait, and two more were also captured on the days that followed. You can use a humane cage trap to catch raccoons and avoid harming them. Take the trapped animals to a wildlife specialist or governmental body in your area. If you want to release them yourself, be extra careful because they may carry rabies. If you get bitten, go to the hospital immediately.

Reinforcing your cages and surrounding your perimeter with electric fences to ward off wolves, coyotes, and foxes is a brilliant investment; however, there are other less obvious methods you can use to protect your flock. For example, you can seal food and keep your trash cans locked up so that you do not attract curious and hungry visitors. A lot of times, predators do not go directly for your fowl but are enticed nearer with food attractions. Therefore, identifying food that ushers in predators and getting rid of it or securing it could be all that it takes to significantly reduce predator populations on your land, which would prevent breaches of your coops.

How your coop was broken into will tell you the animal you are dealing with. Weasels and rats can squeeze through small holes, so there will not be much damage. Foxes and coyotes will make bigger holes in the fencing or weak points of your structure. Bears and wolves will cause massive destruction. Signs of their attacks will be very obvious. If entire birds are missing and no body parts are left while the coop is not damaged, your thieves are likely predator birds. Raccoons can open latches, so if you find your gates open, it is either these masked devils or other humans. Therefore, look at all the details of the breach with an understanding of predator behavior so you can know which solution to explore.

# Chapter 9: Ethics and Best Practices

Ethics can get very complicated due to people having differing views on what is right and wrong, especially when it comes to animals. Different cultural contexts can dictate an appropriate way to treat non-human living beings. There are arguments on whether animals should be farmed at all, especially for meat, considering there is no way for an animal to consent to have its life taken. With all these intersecting dynamics to consider, the goal of acting ethically can be hard to achieve.

**Ethics can get very complicated due to people having differing views on what is right and wrong, especially when it comes to animals.**

To form an ethical system that can be understood and embraced by most compassionate people, you have to delve into the science of animal behavior and psychology. Distressed or ill-treated animals will exhibit physical and social signs of not being well. Some indicators can be measured to determine animal well-being. Based on these, as well as the virtues of kindness and empathy, you can come up with principles that can align with how you should treat animals.

Through the exploration of how the actions of farmers impact poultry, some guidelines can be drafted for you to make sure you are acting ethically. Raising poultry is a huge responsibility, so you should make sure that you are doing it right. Your birds can give you so much, and since you cannot thank them with words, you should show them how grateful you are. Poultry farming ethics underpin the relational exchange you have with your birds. As the person responsible for every aspect of their lives, as well as their ability to reproduce, you should conduct a deep analysis of what would be the most appropriate setup and protocols to have so your birds can enjoy a full and healthy life.

# Defining Poultry Ethics

Poultry farming ethics is all about maximizing the well-being of the animals in your care. Most people acknowledge the sentience of livestock. Animals can feel pain and experience suffering. Farming ethics, therefore, are concerned with eradicating all unnecessary suffering animals experience to live a comfortable life. Cultures across the world have developed standards of bioethics that align with the principle of harm reduction (Macer, 2019). In Ibaraki, Japan, many farmers expressed a deep empathy for their animals but found that they had to balance their caring with economic demands (Macer, 2019). Empathy and morality compel people to consider the treatment of the animals they raise, but that can come into conflict with profit motives, and it becomes quite complex.

The pursuit of maximizing how much money an individual can make has caused some horrific practices to become the standard around the world. Modern society requires walking a tightrope between commercial pressures and the ethical treatment of livestock. To find ways commercial poultry farming could implement ethical standards, Queens University conducted a study about how housing conditions affect the welfare of chickens (O'Connel, 2023). In Australia, no laws enforce the enrichment of housing environments for broiler chickens. This has resulted in the industry adopting farming methods that often cause the animals harm and distress. The large-scale research of Queens University included 40000 chickens (O'Connell, 2023). They found that the simple introduction of windows, perches, and other environment-enhancing equipment significantly reduced aggressive behavior and anxiety while improving the health and physical conditions of the birds (O'Connell, 2023). Even with a profit-motive driving your farming activities, actions can still be taken to reduce harm.

Ethical farming is built on the foundation of having compassion, kindness, and awareness to make changes that improve the lives of your poultry. As much as you are utilizing your birds for meat, eggs, feathers, or companionship, you cannot promote an exploitative relationship where your livestock gain nothing. Most farm animals are selectively bred into existence, which means it is a human choice that their species exist in the numbers that they do. Since people choose to selectively breed animals, it is their responsibility to maximize the physical and psychological well-being of the animals they bring into the world.

If you broadly define poultry farming ethics, they can be described as frameworks that outline the rights of farm birds and the obligations of farmers based on the societal virtues of respect, empathy, compassion, and fairness. Ethics can be a personal commitment, or it could be enforced by law and regulatory bodies. Ethical codes and regulations should be adjusted according to scientific data and new information on what is needed to increase the well-being of livestock. To be an ethical farmer, research what is best for the well-being of your poultry in terms of the changes you need to make to the operation you run, all while advocating for broader shifts in the industry.

Acknowledging that your animals are having a conscious experience that is entirely different from yours but still impactful enough is the beginning of having empathy for animals. Whether you are raising poultry for eggs, feathers, or meat, your animals, on the basis of being able to experience suffering and pleasure, should be given the best life you can reasonably provide. Not many would argue that animal lives have the same value as human lives, but it is essential to acknowledge that they have some intrinsic value, even if it is not the same as a person's. When you work with poultry, you start to see that their experiences, emotions, psychology, and social dynamics are layered and complex. They are not mindless drones just running around; they are engaging with the world with their own form of intelligence.

Poultry ethics can be broken down into a few basic categories:

- Poultry have the right to nutritional food and adequate water.
- Poultry should be allowed to live comfortably in an environment that protects them from injury.
- Poultry should be protected from disease and treated for any ailments or injuries they have.
- Poultry should live in conditions free from emotional and psychological distress.

Every decision you make on your farm should align with these four principles. Once you explore each one, you'll find that there are many subsections to unpack. These principles often overlap, which creates multifaceted solutions. For example, if you combine the principle of providing nutritional food with poultry's right to live comfortably, you may conclude that allowing your birds to feed freely in an open pasture is the most ethical option.

When you farm poultry for profit, food, or as a hobby, you take full responsibility for the welfare of your animals. This gives you a lot more control to make ethical decisions that a mere consumer can't. Poultry meat purchased in stores has labeling that affects consumer decision-making based on morality. However, what the consumer believes is true is often different from the reality on the ground. For example, people may prefer to buy free-range chickens over battery-farmed birds. However, the "free range" label could be misleading because it refers to chickens not kept in battery cages. Free-range chickens can still be kept in dangerously overcrowded conditions. Running your own farm gives you the most moral decision-making power compared to the average consumer.

Acting ethically towards animals is the responsibility of every person on the planet, but once you start raising poultry, you take on additional obligations. Not all birds are the same. You do not raise chickens in the same way you raise ducks or turkeys. Therefore, ethical actions are catered to the unique position and structure of your farm. You have to deeply understand your animals so that you can make the correct choices for their well-being. Ethics are not always black and white and often fall into grey areas, especially when it comes to livestock, because so many cultures have wildly varying views on what is right or wrong. Although some clear ethical standards should be upheld, your values will determine how you align with them in the small details of your operation. To measure whether your farm protocols adequately ensure the well-being of your animals and provide them with dignity, you must assess the impact of your actions.

## The Impact of Choice

The choices you make for your birds will affect the quality of their entire lives. Sometimes, a misunderstanding of what your choices cause can result in you taking a path that exponentially increases the suffering of your animals. Various species of poultry have complicated social hierarchies, biology, and psychological processes. Small actions could have a huge impact on your birds. If you do not understand the impact of your actions on their physical and emotional well-being, you could take paths that leave your beloved animals in constant distress.

When compassion and kindness are not the foundation of your farm, it is easy to slip into a spiral of inhumane activities. For example, turkeys do not thrive in overcrowded conditions. If turkeys do not have enough space, they become violently aggressive. Having aggressive turkeys in a small space leads to many fights as the birds get into each other's way. Commercial turkey farmers usually keep the birds in lower light because it reduces their aggression, which adversely affects their eyes, causing defects and blindness. Turkeys can also become cannibalistic in crowded conditions. The constant fighting and cannibalism cause some farms to remove their beaks to reduce injury. The first unethical practice of overcrowding directly caused two more unethical actions, namely, damaging the turkeys' eyes with low light and mutilating their bodies to make fights less deadly. Cruelty is a slippery slope that exponentially multiplies negative outcomes.

Sometimes, consumer demand facilitates unethical choices for farmers. Foie gras is the French delicacy of fatty duck liver. This dish is served in many top restaurants around the world and can be ridiculously expensive. The fatty liver comes from ducks kept in constrictive cages and force-fed through a pipe to achieve the flavorful liver texture that foie gras enjoyers love. As a poultry farmer, you could probably make a lot of profit by exploiting this niche market. Your choice to participate in the industry because of the consumer demand directly increases the suffering of ducks. You will need to weigh the ethics of valuing the comfortable life of your ducks with obtaining insane profits selling the high-class delicacy.

Ethics is not a zero-sum game and typically works with a sliding scale. Some practices are better than others, but that does not mean they are cruelty-free or even ideal. This becomes apparent when you look at battery-farmed chickens compared to their cageless alternatives. In battery cages, the cramped conditions prevent hens from exhibiting many of their natural behaviors, like nesting, perching, and dustbathing. This causes increased frustration and stress, which could lead to some physical symptoms like feather loss and a weaker body. Their cageless counterparts are allowed to spread their wings and move around freely, so in terms of managing emotional and psychological distress, this option is by all means superior.

This does not mean that cageless farming is ethical. Many of the same practices that happen in battery farming are replicated in cageless farming. On egg farms, many breeders kill male chicks because they are not economically viable to raise. These chicks are often burnt alive, drowned, or even put into plastic bags to rot. Both cage-free and battery farms purchase chicks from breeders, where this unethical practice is the norm. Moreover, both cage-free and battery chickens have their beaks cut off and are usually slaughtered long before they reach adulthood. Therefore, although cage-free chicken farming is better, it is still not ethical.

If you were to choose between cage-free chickens or battery chickens based solely on ethical evaluations, you would probably go with the former, even though it is unethical when using a black-and-white lens. Furthermore, some practices that are considered to be morally correct today could be completely abhorrent in the next ten years based on new research that emerges and the direction in which society moves. The greyness of ethical dilemmas is unavoidable. Being too rigid in your ethical standards can hold you back in many ways. It can be frustratingly difficult to determine which path is the best option for raising poultry.

It is hard to make an immediate transition from unethical to ethical, considering that the concept of ethics can be so amorphous and abstract. You live in a world filled with questionable and downright immoral actions written into many of the systems and institutions that form society. When you start making ethical considerations, especially as they relate to farming, you will quickly notice that you must make gradual steps toward allowing your farm to align with the values of kindness and compassion. Some people may argue that the practice of raising animals is itself unethical, so reaching 100% purity in poultry farming may be an impossible pursuit. You must approach your ethics as a constant mission to align with your virtues and moral systems. Take an animal-centered approach where you value your birds beyond commodities as living beings. Work on transforming your yard into a turkey, duck, chicken, or guinea paradise by studying their behavior, observing their responses to the environment, and looking at their health outcomes.

When you look at birds that were raised in a healthy environment with a farmer who is deeply concerned about ethical practices and compare them to a factory farm that only cares about ethics as it relates to staying within the bounds of the law, the differences are stark. Many people see their neatly packed chickens on their plates, but they never get to see how they were treated while they were alive. It is reasonable to assume that if some people saw the treatment of animals on factory farms, they would think twice about the meat they purchase. Humanity as a collective is participating in a project to move the world to a more ethical place. This shows up in all the systems of law and morality that people embrace. One of the frontiers of improving the world is how people treat nature and animals. It is impossible to undo all the cruel practices that have been embraced as the norm with one backyard farm. The small changes you make in your life and the ideas you advocate for will push the farming industry into a more caring position.

# Beyond the Backyard

The ethics you have on your farm do not stop at your gate. There is a whole industry and supply chain linked to all the actions you take on your farm, including sourcing your animals and acquiring feed. Where you buy your poultry from is crucial for embracing more humane ways of farming. It does not help to have a humane farm while you support breeders who have no regard for ethics. For example, some breeders that sell egg-laying hens kill the male chicks because they are not as profitable. Other breeders genetically manipulate broilers so that they can grow faster, but this has the adverse effect of the chickens developing deformities and chronic diseases. Unnecessary suffering begins where you get your animal from.

The next step in the poultry farming supply chain to consider is where you get your feed from. The life quality of your birds is not the only ethical concern you should have as a poultry farmer. If your values are based on compassion, you cannot ignore your environmental impact because there are a multitude of living beings directly impacted by how you engage with this planet. The grains grown to feed your chickens may have been produced using chemicals and practices that degrade the soil and destabilize local ecosystems. Therefore, growing your own feed or sourcing organic produce is a way to be ethical beyond the gates of your farm.

Your advocacy for the restructuring and improvement of the commercial farming industry is one of the most important things you can do to stretch your ethical arms beyond the confines of your property. Making changes in the way you raise poultry is powerful for spreading interspecies kindness, but you are only one farmer in a giant pool. To reform the industry, you need to get many more people on board with the vision of compassion that you have. Your activism is needed to change the minds of farmers stuck in the status quo of the industry and to apply pressure on lawmakers and regulatory bodies to enforce new rules for systematic change.

Although it is not always possible, try as best you can to source your animals and the products you use for poultry farming from local producers. The carbon footprint of sourcing locally is significantly lower than that of products that are shipped in. Moreover, you will likely support small businesses and local economies that keep mom-and-pop stores alive. If your ethics stem from your virtues, you should also extend them to your economic decision-making. The choices you make with your purchases impact the environment and society, so you should be mindful of what you buy and where you buy it.

You do not need to advocate for your feathered friends alone. Multiple NGOs, NPOs, and other activist organizations are already working toward making the world a better place for farm animals. You can also join online communities to amplify the message. It may seem daunting, but when you become active, your small contribution will add momentum to the movement, creating a rapid snowball effect. Every kind farmer should be an advocate for the well-being of animals. You may want to treat your animals right because you have a personal connection with them. Use that empathy as a motivating force because if you understand the bonds you have with your birds, you should be able to conclude that other poultry deserve the same. As long as there are birds who are not experiencing the anguish-free life you provide, your work is not done.

# Chapter 10: Beyond the Basics: Rarer Breeds and Conservation

In this chapter, you'll delve into the fascinating world of some of the rarest poultry breeds. You'll find out about the intricacies that contribute to the rarity of these birds, learning their distinctive traits, captivating histories, and close encounters with extinction. Moving forward, you'll also explore the significance of conservation and the efforts it requires.

## Meet the Rare Gems

### 1. Dong Tao

One of the most unusual chickens you will ever see is the Dong Tao, also referred to as the Dragon Chicken.

One of the most unusual chickens you will ever see is the Dong Tao, also referred to as the Dragon Chicken. They are quite big, and the roosters weigh over 12 lbs., whereas the hens weigh around 9 lbs. The Dong Tao features brilliant red wattles and ear lobes on a pea comb. The hens' feathers are off-white in color, while the roosters are red with black breasts. Their thick and scaly crimson legs can grow to the width of a man's wrist. Because the hens have a tendency to smash their eggs, mechanical incubation is typically used to raise the chicks. These breeds only lay eggs for 2 to 3 months and then rest for a while before getting back at it. This is why they are called the cyclical layers. They lay up to 60 eggs a year. This breed is calm, friendly, and good-natured. These uncommon chickens, which are prized as delicacies in Vietnam, were originally reared exclusively for royal consumption. These days, a pair of Dong Tao can for over two thousand dollars.

## 2. Sultan

This rare breed can be found in three colors: blue, white, and black.
https://commons.wikimedia.org/wiki/File:Tab41_H%C3%BChner_(Gefl%C3%BCgel-Album,_Jean_Bungartz,_1885).jpg

A Sultan is a sight to be admired. The vulture hocks, long tail, dropped wings, muffs, head crest, large nares, and the V-comb are just a few of its exquisite traits. This rare breed can be found in three colors: blue, white, and black. White is the most well-known and easy-to-find breed. The blue variety is incredibly rare. These hens, which date back to the 14th century in the Ottoman Empire, were housed as decorative birds in the Sultan's residence. In Turkish, they are known as Serai Tavuk, which translates to "fowl of the Sultan's palace." The roosters can weigh up to 6 lbs, whereas the hens may weigh up to 4 lbs. They also come in even rarer bantam sizes! Seeing how they are poor layers, the hens can only lay two eggs per week. They make for wonderful house chickens and are purely ornamental.

### 3. Brabanter

This is one of the oldest breeds, dating back to around 1676. It was developed in the historic Brabant area, and that is where it gets its name. They are pretty small and weigh around 4 to 5 lbs. only. The hens may weigh even less. These are not like your typical birds. They have no wattles, large and wide nostrils, a beard, and a crest. They come in a variety of colors, which include cuckoo, gold, and silver spangled. They can lay up to 3 large eggs in a week and love to free-range. These birds are smart, friendly, calm, and shy. They are rarely, if ever, unhappy. It's fascinating to note that enthusiasts were able to save these hens from extinction at the beginning of the 20th century. However, they are still quite rare and in need of conservation efforts.

### 4. La Fleche

Its name, which means "arrow," comes from the French town of La Fleche, which is near Le Mans.

La Fleche was an extremely popular table bird in the fifteenth century. Its name, which means "arrow," comes from the French town of La Fleche, which is near Le Mans. This chicken grows quite slowly and takes around ten months to grow enough to be sold. Its slow growth is the reason why this wonderful chicken has become so rare. They lay around three large white eggs per week, or 180 eggs per year on average. The species, known as the Devil species, has a peculiar appearance with a V-shaped comb. The roosters are about eight pounds in weight. The hens are too heavy for city living—they weigh more than 6.5 pounds. They also like to fly a little bit and roam freely. Although uncommon, this bird is starting to repopulate.

## 5. Old English Pheasant Fowl

The Old English Pheasant is a historic English breed of poultry.

The Old English Pheasant is a historic English breed of poultry. They were made from various utility poultry varieties and were once fairly common on farms in Yorkshire and Lancashire. Many of these old types of pheasant fowl were absorbed into the Hamburg breed. Some bird enthusiasts searched around the country for ones that had not been absorbed. This is why, in 1914, the birds were named Old English Pheasant fowl to ensure that they were protected. They are energetic and flighty breeds that love to run wild and would not appreciate closed spaces at all. Their feathers are brown and black. The feathering acts as a camouflage and protects them from predators while they are free-ranging. These birds are good layers and produce around 3 to 4 eggs per week and around 160 to 220 medium-sized eggs per year. They are not very broody and make for wonderful mothers to their chicks. Due to its rare dual-purpose nature, this is an ideal bird for homesteads.

## 6. Breda

It appears in artworks dating back to 1660, where they are shown as farm animals.
https://commons.wikimedia.org/wiki/File:Tab19_H%C3%BChner_(Gefl%C3%BCgel-Album,_Jean_Bungartz,_1885).jpg

The Netherlands is home to the historic breed of Breda chicken. It appears in artworks dating back to 1660, where they are shown as farm animals. It is known by many names, including Crow heads, Kraaikops, and Guelderlands. They were quite popular in the US during the Civil War; however, they lost their popularity until they became completely extinct from the US in the 1800s. The Dutch maintained this breed, but its numbers were quickly declining there as well. This chicken is friendly and alert but calm. Free-ranging is one of its favorite things, and it prefers to stay around its house after its daily walkabouts. With its vulture hocks and feathery legs, the Breda stands erect. It has muscular thighs. It is capable of a fantastic standing leap when startled. Because it lacks a comb, it works well in chilly areas. Its head contains a few feather tufts, albeit they are not very noticeable. It features little red wattles and white earlobes. Its nares are large, just like the Brabanter.

## 7. Onagadori

**This rare breed is famous for its unusually long tail.**

Onagadori was first bred in the seventeenth century in the Kochi District of Japan. This rare breed is famous for its unusually long tail. In 1952, it was regarded as a National Natural Treasure of Japan. The longest tail recorded was an amazing 88ft long (27m). Only a rooster's tail is able to grow this long as the hen's feathering is similar to that of other chickens, and it will not grow that much. Sadly, only 250 chickens are estimated to exist now, and it is purely an ornamental breed. The hens lay over 80 to 100 brown eggs but are not sitters. Breeding it requires a lot of experience. You will only want to give this rare bird a chance if you're a seasoned breeder. Their coop and run must be big enough and should be kept clean. Its perches should also be placed high to protect its tail.

## 8. Burmese

The Burmese bantam chicken is probably the rarest one in existence today. It has been staggering on the brink of extinction for decades now. It was considered extinct at one point until a small flock was discovered in the 1970s. It was not the most fertile bird, and it had to breed with other similar breeds. One of them is Barbu D'Uccles. This practice revitalized the breed, and the flock has continued to grow gradually. The Burmese are regarded as real bantams and have a single comb with a little crest of head feathers. The roosters weigh around 600g, and hens weigh over 500g. Their legs are bright yellow with feathers, and they have vulture hocks with white plumage. Their legs are unusually short, and it is caused by a "creeper" gene that also causes high mortality in embryos. That is also why this bird has become so rare. This breed is quite old, as is mentioned in one of Charles Darwin's books (The Variation of Plants and Animals under Domestication). The hens lay 3 small brown eggs each week and make for great mothers of broody. Overall, it is a friendly and quiet bird that makes up a great backyard flock.

## 9. Scots Dumpy

DUMPIES, BELONGING TO J. FAIRLIE, ESQ.

These birds originated from Scotland and are an endangered breed.

These birds originated from Scotland and are an endangered breed. This breed gets its name from the creeper gene that gives them really short legs. They have also been referred to as Crawlers or Creepers. Unfortunately, this gene has caused many embryo deaths. Before a small flock was found in Kenya and brought back to the UK, it was believed that they had gone extinct in 1970. Scots Dumpys are a dual-purpose breed that loves to free range. It lays around 3 eggs per week and makes for excellent mothers. They consist of four color varieties: silver grey, black, cuckoo, and dark. Seeing how it's endangered, this rare breed is in severe need of protection.

## 10. Magpie Ducks

These active and docile birds are decorative, have great egg layers, and are known for their meat.
*Stephen James McWilliam, CC BY 4.0 <https://creativecommons.org/licenses/by/4.0>, via Wikimedia Commons: https://commons.wikimedia.org/wiki/File:Magpie_Duck,_drake_(cropped).jpg*

Magpies were recognized in 1977 by the APA (American Poultry Association). They weigh 4 to 4.5 lbs. and lay medium to large white eggs. These active and docile birds are decorative, have great egg layers, and are known for their meat. They are also known for their white plumage, with a few specific marks on their crown and body (from the shoulders to the tail). Those markings are usually black and blue. Some breeders have developed other colors like chocolate and silver. It is important to note that their markings do not change colors when they mature; this allows the breeders to choose utility birds and breeding stock when they are young. If you are looking for breeding stock, select strong-legged and active birds that come from high-egg production families. Keep in mind that their ability to lay eggs and the size of those eggs are significantly influenced by high-producing families.

## 11. Jersey Buff Turkey

The Jersey Buff turkey is a rare, striking, buff-colored bird with black, white, and brown feathers. It originated from the mid-Atlantic region and is also known as the Buff Turkey. In 1874, the American Poultry Association (APA) approved this breed. They weigh from 12 to 21 lbs.

The hens weigh about 12 lbs., whereas the toms can weigh up to 21 lbs. These birds can be either docile or aggressive. The hens lay pale cream to medium brown colored eggs with spotting. The Buff Turkey is ideal for hobby or small-scale farms. They are mainly bred for meat production. It can be a costly bird. A 16 lbs. Jersey Buff Turkey can go for around $349.99. Its meat is in high demand.

## 12. Cotton Patch Geese

In most, the males are mostly white, whereas the females are mostly dove gray to brownish with white variances in their feathers.

*Kororaa, CC BY-SA 3.0 <https://creativecommons.org/licenses/by-sa/3.0>, via Wikimedia Commons: https://commons.wikimedia.org/wiki/File:Cotton_Patch_Goose.jpg*

The Cotton Patch is a light to medium-sized, upright bird. It has an elongated body and is less rounded than other breeds like Pilgrim goose or Shetland. Cotton Patch geese have rounded heads, blue eyes, an orange-pink beak, and feet. It has a minimal paunch and, when present, a single lobe. In most, the males are mostly white, whereas the females are mostly dove gray to brownish with white variances in their feathers. The geese can lay up to 4 to 7 eggs per clutch. The eggs are large and white in color. The ganders can weigh around 9 to 12 lbs., whereas the geese weigh up to 8 to 10 lbs. These birds are great flyers, which helps them escape predators, but that may not be a great quality to some breeders. These birds are great foragers, and thanks to their small size, they can survive extremely hot weather.

## 13. Saxony Ducks

Saxony ducks are wonderful, easygoing birds that can adapt to all sorts of environments. Their eggs are extra-large and may be white or blue-green in color. They are large, all-purpose birds and can weigh around 6 to 8 lbs. One of their best qualities is their calm and docile nature. Saxony ducks are wonderful foragers and reduce the number of snails and slugs around.

## 14. KellyBronze Turkey

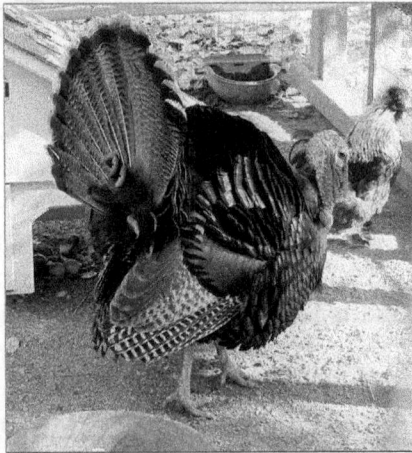

KellyBronze Turkey has one of the most expensive meats and is greatly celebrated by celebrity chefs. It is sold for around $12 per pound, which means that a fully adult bird may cost around $300. It has delicate and moist meat. It takes half the time to cook than a regular turkey and is naturally juicy. If they are allowed to forage for themselves and roam freely, they'll produce that highly sought-after meat. It is a slow-growing breed and takes a long time to get to the right weight. Its maturity has a significant impact on the flavor. The hens lay eggs in spring and only lay for 10 weeks.

## Conservation: Why It Matters

Conserving poultry breeds has multiple ecological implications. It is mainly related to environmental sustainability, biodiversity, and the preservation of genetic resources. Here is a list of some key considerations:

### Environmental Sustainability

The poultry breed has evolved in different geographic areas and has adapted to various environments. There is a need to conserve these breeds in order to ensure that the industry remains resilient when it comes to environmental challenges like climate change. It is also essential to understand that some of these traditional breeds may have developed resistance to certain diseases. These traits can only be conserved if these species are taken care of.

### Biodiversity Preservation

Conservation of various poultry breeds helps with maintaining a diverse genetic pool. This is especially important for fighting against illnesses, environmental changes, or other issues. This diverse group also contributes to the overall biodiversity in agriculture. It is extremely important for the broader ecosystem as these diverse agricultural systems support many other organisms like insects, plants, fungi, etc.

### Sustainable Agriculture Practices

Native poultry breeds play a huge role in sustainable farming practices as they do not require any external inputs such as special diets or medication, leading to a sustainable and environmentally friendly agricultural system. Moreover, maintaining a variety of poultry breeds can prevent overreliance on certain highly specialized breeds. Diversity may be able to reduce the impact of large-scale industrial poultry farming.

### Cultural and Heritage Conservation

Many poultry breeds have local and cultural significance. By preserving these breeds, you maintain the connection between people and their agricultural history. It also helps support local economies, especially in areas where the traditional breed has a significant impact on the livelihood of those communities.

### Education and Awareness

You can highlight the importance of sustainable agricultural practices and biodiversity to create awareness among friends, farmers, decision-makers, and the public.

# Getting Involved

You can also learn how you can help and make active efforts towards the conservation of the environment. It is a collective responsibility to take care of the wildlife habitat to ensure that all the threatened species are not harmed. Everyone must take conscious steps to ensure that their best interests are prioritized. Here's how you can get involved:

### 1. Learning about the Endangered Species in Your Region

The first step toward conserving the environment is learning about the amazing wildlife around you. You must find everything you can about the endangered species in your region and learn what makes them interesting and why they are so important. The natural world has provided you with benefits, including clean air, food, water, and even medicines. It is your duty to pay back and protect the environment.

### 2. Give Back by Volunteering

Try your best to visit and volunteer at wildlife parks. Protected spaces keep native wildlife, including plants, birds, and fish safe. The best way to protect endangered species is to protect the environment. These dedicated places create many wildlife-related jobs for thousands of people and help businesses support the environment.

### 3. Make Your Backyard Wildlife-Friendly

You should try your best to make your home a safe space for wildlife. Keep your garbage cans closed. Lock your pets in at night and feed them inside to avoid attracting wild animals. You must also make an effort to disinfect the bird baths to avoid disease transmission. Sadly, a large number of birds die as a result of collisions with windows. You can also reduce the number by putting decals on your windows.

#### 4. Native Wildlife Rely on the Native Plants

You should try your best to allow native plants to fully grow. You can pollinate your plants by attracting bees and butterflies. Unfortunately, the spread of non-native species has significantly impacted the native populations around the globe. These species are usually invasive and compete with the native species for habitat and resources. They can also force the surrounding native species into extinction.

#### 5. Avoid Pesticides

Although insecticides and herbicides can keep your backyard healthy and looking great, their contents are extremely detrimental to wildlife. These chemicals take a long time to degrade and may build up in the soil, affecting the food chain. Predators like owls, coyotes, and hawks can also get harmed if they consume poisoned prey. Keep in mind that amphibians are especially vulnerable to these pollutants and can greatly suffer if exposed to high levels of pesticides.

#### 6. Drive Responsibly

Drive carefully and under the speed limit to avoid harming wild animals. Roads are especially dangerous for wildlife.

#### 7. Recycle

Pay attention to what you consume, and always recycle. Make an effort to buy recycled and sustainable products to reduce your carbon footprint. Never buy furniture made from wood procured from rainforests. Also, the mineral used in cellphones and other electronics is mined in gorilla habitats; this is why it is important to recycle your mobile phones and other appliances. Also, try to limit the use of palm oil as tiger habitats are being destroyed to make more room for plantations.

#### 8. Do Not Interfere with Wildlife

Interfering with wildlife by shooting, trapping, or forcing into captivity is illegal and can lead to endangered species going extinct. If you come across someone doing any of those things, contact the local wildlife enforcement office.

#### 9. Do Not Buy Products Made from Endangered Species

This goes without saying, but never buy anything made from an endangered species. Going on trips abroad is an exhilarating experience, and it makes you want to collect souvenirs. However, avoid anything made from tortoise shells, coral, or ivory. You should also never buy products made from endangered species like tigers, sea otters, polar bears, crocodile skin, and parrots.

## 10. Protect Habitats

Wildlife habitats are being destroyed rapidly, which poses a major threat to many species. The best way to protect threatened species is by protecting where they live. They should have access to resources to raise their young and find food and shelter. Petition the local authorities if you hear of any oil and gas drilling, logging, and overgrazing near wildlife.

# Conclusion

Taking the first step to start a poultry farm may not be the most difficult, but it is the most daunting. Jumping into the unknown will always be scary. You now have the basic knowledge you need to get started. Remember, you need to match the birds you want to raise to your property. Not every fowl will do well in all environments. You then must set up adequate housing that caters to all their needs. For example, if you are raising ducks, you need a body of water nearby. If you have chickens or turkeys, they need ample space to move around and places to perch.

From nutrition to the health and wellness of your animals, you are well prepared to embark on this amazing journey. Whether you are farming poultry for food or just as a hobby, dealing with livestock is not child's play. Once your farm becomes productive and you get that first feather harvest or gather that initial dozen eggs, the joy you will feel is unrivaled. However, the life of a poultry farmer has a lot of ups and downs. You need to brace yourself for a wild ride. A disease could spread through your flock, or a predator could rip through your cages. You must be resilient and prepared enough to take some hits along the way.

Farming can never be selfish. You are dedicating your time and effort to the well-being of helpless animals. Compared to domesticated dogs and cats, the connection that can be cultivated for other species is often underrated. As you spend time with your birds, you will begin noticing their behavior and unique personalities. You might even develop a bond with a few that will become your favorites. This bond should inspire you to act within the bounds of ethical practices and even take steps for the sake of conservation. Given that Earth supports all life, you should care for it like you care for your birds. If you are breeding protected species, remember that there is a big responsibility on your shoulders. You also need to make sure that you function within legal frameworks to stay out of trouble.

Transforming your homestead, yard, plot, or commercial farm into a poultry paradise will take a lot of elbow grease. Getting down into the dirt is exciting and can awaken something primal in you. If you look after them well, your birds will respect your efforts and return the favor bountifully. Good luck on your poultry adventure, and take the time to refresh your mind with the tips and techniques you find throughout this book whenever you feel lost or confused.

# Here's another book by Dion Rosser that you might like

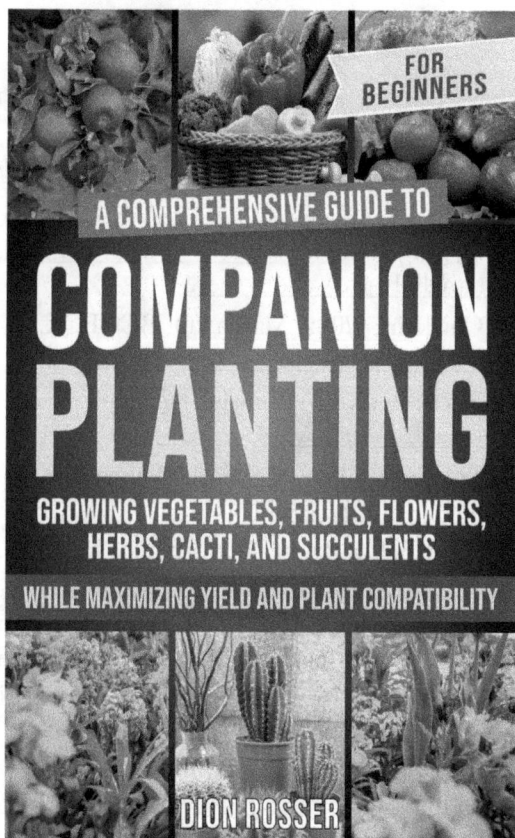

FOR BEGINNERS

A COMPREHENSIVE GUIDE TO

# COMPANION PLANTING

GROWING VEGETABLES, FRUITS, FLOWERS, HERBS, CACTI, AND SUCCULENTS

WHILE MAXIMIZING YIELD AND PLANT COMPATIBILITY

DION ROSSER

# References

10 Facts about Geese. (2019, April 9). FOUR PAWS International - Animal Welfare Organisation; #organization. https://www.four-paws.org/campaigns-topics/topics/farm-animals/10-facts-about-geese

10 Fun Facts about Chickens. (2022, March 26). BC SPCA. https://spca.bc.ca/news/fun-facts-about-chickens/

10 Incredible Duck Facts. (n.d).AZ Animals. https://a-z-animals.com/blog/incredible-duck-facts/

10 Turkey Facts. (2020, September 28). World Animal Protection. https://www.worldanimalprotection.us/blogs/10-turkey-facts

15 Management Tips for Better Poultry Performance Potential. (2018, June 21).Alltech. https://www.alltech.com/blog/15-management-tips-better-poultry-performance-potential

7 Benefits to Raising Backyard Chickens. (2022, October 31). Strombergs. https://www.strombergschickens.com/blog/7-benefits-to-raising-backyard-chickens/

7 Therapeutic Benefits of Birdwatching. (n.d.). Careuk.com. https://www.careuk.com/company/care-uk-campaigns/bird-watch/7-therapeutic-benefits-of-birdwatching

Ajaero, T. M. (2018, February 8). How to Care for Baby Chicks After they Hatch. ProfitableVenture; Profitable Venture Magazine Ltd. https://www.profitableventure.com/care-for-baby-chicks-hatch/

Amorvet is a Poultry Feed Supplement Manufacturer. (2023, July 27). Amorvet. https://www.amorvet.com/blogs/poultryfeedsupplement/

April. (2022, April 18). 5 Most Expensive Turkey Breeds. The Hip Chick. https://thehipchick.com/expensive-turkey-breeds/

Are Treats for Chickens Good for your Flock's Health? (n.d.). Raising Happy Chickens. https://www.raising-happy-chickens.com/treats-for-chickens.html

Atapattu, S., & Baker, A. (n.d.). SOLID BROILER MANAGEMENT Training Manual. https://pdf.usaid.gov/pdf_docs/pa00mgpt.pdf

Basic Duck Care. (2020, February 17). Cornell University College of Veterinary Medicine. https://www.vet.cornell.edu/animal-health-diagnostic-center/programs/duck-research-lab/basic-duck-care

Basic Poultry Nutrition. (n.d.). Extension.org. https://poultry.extension.org/articles/feeds-and-feeding-of-poultry/basic-poultry-nutrition/

Benefits of Poultry Feed Supplements. (2021, January 12). Shivam Chemicals Limited. https://www.shivamchem.com/blog/benefits-of-poultry-feed-supplements/

Berg, C. (2002). Health and Welfare in Organic Poultry Production. Acta Veterinaria Scandinavica, 43(Suppl 1), S37. https://doi.org/10.1186/1751-0147-43-s1-s37

bestnestbox.com. (2015, August 12). Interested In Raising Chickens? Here Are Some Common Myths About Chicken Farming, Debunked: Part 1. Bestnestbox.com. https://bestnestbox.com/blogs/news/common-myths-about-chicken-farming-debunked-part-1

bestnestbox.com. (2015, August 15). Interested In Raising Chickens? Here Are Some Common Myths About Chicken Farming, Debunked: Part 2. Bestnestbox.com. https://bestnestbox.com/blogs/news/interested-in-raising-chickens-here-are-some-common-myths-about-chicken-farming-debunked-part-2

Bird Food Guide: An Insider's Guide to the Ideal Avian Diet. (2012, April 7). Lafeber® Pet Birds.

Branaman, J. (2018). Cage-free vs. battery-cage eggs. The Humane Society of the United States. https://www.humanesociety.org/resources/cage-free-vs-battery-cage-eggs

Brian. (2015, March 11). 5 Common Misconceptions about Raising Chickens for Meat. Ferrin Brook Farm. https://ferrinbrookfarm.wordpress.com/2015/03/11/5-common-misconceptions-about-raising-chickens-for-meat-2/

British Hen Welfare Trust. (2022, September 21). A Guide to Chicken Treats; Everything in Moderation. British Hen Welfare Trust. https://www.bhwt.org.uk/blog/health-welfare/chicken-treats-guide/

Bronze, K. (2019, November 8). More than Just a Turkey - Kelly Bronze. KellyBronze. https://www.kellybronze.co.uk/more-than-just-a-turkey/

Bupp, J. (2022, November 13). Defending Our Chickens Against Four-Legged Thieves. Lancasterfarming.com. https://www.lancasterfarming.com/country-life/family/defending-our-chickens-against-four-legged-theives/article_82c4dd2a-6098-11ed-87af-8b31b24e30d2.html

Capps, A. (2014, November 21). These Amazing Conversations Between Turkeys & Humans may Change Your Mind about Eating Them. Free From Harm. https://freefromharm.org/videos/turkey-talk/

Carlson, R. E. (2023, October 11). Advantages and disadvantages of free range chickens: What you need to know. Homesteading Simple Self-Sufficiency Off-The-Grid | Homesteading.com. \

Chicken. (2016, April 25). Smithsonian's National Zoo; Smithsonian's National Zoo and Conservation Biology Institute. https://nationalzoo.si.edu/animals/domestic-chicken

Cole, T. (2019, February 22). Poultry houses: 197 designs, structures, plans & systems (PDF guide). The Big Book Project. https://thebigbookproject.org/agri/poultry-farming/houses-chicken/

Coogan, K. (2023, November 16). Four rare and threatened duck breeds. Backyard Poultry. https://backyardpoultry.iamcountryside.com/poultry-101/four-threatened-duck-breeds/

Country Smallholding. (2016, May 9). Chicken body language. Country Smallholding. https://thecountrysmallholder.com/country-smallholding/chicken-body-language-6260096/

Daniel. (2020, December 17). 7 Different Types of Poultry Birds. Agricfy.com. https://agricfy.com/types-of-poultry/

Daniels, T. (2012, May 8). The Beginner's Guide to Keeping Geese. Poultrykeeper.com; Tim Daniels. https://poultrykeeper.com/keeping-geese/beginners-guide-keeping-geese/

DeVore, S. (2019, April 5). Forage or Feed? Nutritional Benefits of Chickens that Forage. News From The Coop. https://newsfromthecoop.hoovershatchery.com/forage-or-feed-best-for-chickens-nutritional-benefits-of-chickens-that-forage/

Discover 11 Fascinating Pigeon Facts. (2022, March 9). Excel Pest Services. https://www.excelpestservices.com/11-fun-facts-about-pigeons/

Disease Control And Management. (n.d.). Tnau.Ac.In. http://www.agritech.tnau.ac.in/expert_system/poultry/

Diseases of poultry. (n.d.). Msstate.edu. https://extension.msstate.edu/agriculture/livestock/poultry/diseases-poultry

Duck. (2019, October 5). Animal Spot. https://www.animalspot.net/duck

Endangered. (2020, October 2). 10 Easy Things You Can Do to Save Endangered Species. Endangered Species Coalition.

https://www.endangered.org/10-easy-things-you-can-do-to-save-endangered-species/

Farhat, G. (2023, April 6). An Evaluation of Different Chicken Housing Systems. MonoGutHealth. https://monoguthealth.eu/an-evaluation-of-different-chicken-housing-systems-2/

Farm, R. (2023, November 6). Jersey Buff Turkey: Characteristics & Best 7 facts. ROYS FARM. https://www.roysfarm.com/jersey-buff-turkey/

Farm. (2018, April 2). 9 Basic Considerations for Backyard Poultry. Farm and Dairy. https://www.farmanddairy.com/top-stories/9-basic-considerations-for-backyard-poultry/478093.html

Feed Additives for use in Poultry Diets | Animal & Food Sciences. https://afs.ca.uky.edu/poultry/feed-additives-use-poultry-diets

Feed additives. (n.d.). Food Safety. https://food.ec.europa.eu/safety/animal-feed/feed-additives_en

Feed Ingredients. (n.d.). Poultry Hub Australia. https://www.poultryhub.org/all-about-poultry/nutrition/feed-ingredients

Flank, L. (2017, September 8). Chicken Behavior: The Politics of the Pecking Order. Hobby Farms. https://www.hobbyfarms.com/pecking-order-chicken-behavior-history-science/

Foie Gras: Cruelty to Ducks and Geese. (2010, June 22). PETA. https://www.peta.org/issues/animals-used-for-food/factory-farming/ducks-geese/foie-gras/

Freedomrangerhatchery. (2022, July 7). Raising Turkeys 101 | Freedom Ranger Hatcheries. https://www.freedomrangerhatchery.com/blog/raising-turkeys-101-how-to-grow-happy-healthy-poults/

Fromm, I. (2018, October 23). 15 Fun Facts about Chickens. Carolinacoops.com. https://carolinacoops.com/resources/15-fun-facts-about-chickens/

Garrigus, W. P. (2023). Poultry Farming. In Encyclopedia Britannica.

Goldman, J. G. (n.d.). Nothing To Gobble At: Social Cognition in Turkeys. Scientific American Blog Network. https://blogs.scientificamerican.com/thoughtful-animal/nothing-to-gobble-at-social-cognition-in-turkeys/

Gomez, M. (2023, July 30). 10 Quail Facts about the Stout Small Pheasants. TRVST. https://www.trvst.world/biodiversity/quail-facts/

Haberfield, J. (2021, August 3). Pigeon & Dove Care – Learn How To Take Care of These Birds. The Unusual Pet Vets. https://www.unusualpetvets.com.au/pigeon-and-dove-care/

Hayes, B. (2022, February 4). 11 Benefits of Raising Chickens You Didn't Know. Homesteading Where You Are. https://www.homesteadingwhereyouare.com/2022/02/03/benefits-of-raising-chickens/

Health and welfare. (2020, July 20). Agriculture Victoria. https://agriculture.vic.gov.au/livestock-and-animals/poultry-and-eggs/health-and-welfare

Hotaling, A. (2021, June 30). Common Myths About the Backyard Chicken Flock. Hobby Farms. https://www.hobbyfarms.com/common-myths-about-the-backyard-chicken-flock/

How To Deal With an Aggressive Rooster. (n.d.). Raising Happy Chickens. https://www.raising-happy-chickens.com/aggressive-rooster.html

How to Read Turkeys' Body Language. (2020). Montanadecoy.com. https://montanadecoy.com/blog/how-to-read-a-turkeys-body-language/

Identifying 12 Backyard Chicken Predators. (2018, September 19). Predator Guard. https://predatorguard.com/blogs/news/identifying-12-backyard-chicken-predators

Ingram, B. (2019, November 6).Meet the Alpha Hen: Every Flock Has One. Hobby Farms. https://www.hobbyfarms.com/meet-the-alpha-hen-every-flock-has-one/

Ito, D., & Hendrix, H. (2021, April 7). Changing poultry housing systems, having the right breed for the right system - Laying Hens. https://layinghens.hendrix-genetics.com/en/news/changing-poultry-housing-systems-having-the-right-breed-for-the-right-housing-system/

Jagdish. (2020, November 28). Poultry Housing – Types, Equipment, and Construction. Agri Farming. https://www.agrifarming.in/poultry-housing-types-equipment-and-construction

Johnsgard, P. A. (1968). The Evolution of Duck Courtship . University of Nebraska-Lincoln. https://digitalcommons.unl.edu/cgi/viewcontent.cgi?article=1030&context=biosciornithology

Kubala, J., MS, & RD. (2022, April 8). How To Raise Chickens: A Complete Beginner's Guide. Healthline. https://www.healthline.com/nutrition/how-to-raise-chickens

Kunzmann, P. (2011, September 7). Ethics in the Poultry Industry – Answering Moral Questions of Society.Lohmann Breeders. https://lohmann-breeders.com/lohmanninfo/ethics-in-the-poultry-industry-answering-moral-questions-of-society/

Lesley, C. (2020, August 9). The 9 Rarest Chicken Breeds In The World. Chickens And More. https://www.chickensandmore.com/rare-chicken-breeds/

Lie-Nielsen, K. (2017, November 17). Questions Before you Get Geese. Hostilevalleyliving. https://www.hostilevalleyliving.com/single-post/2017/11/17/questions-before-you-get-geese

LineaPoultry Predator Identification: A Guide to Tracks and Sign. (2015, March 15). Ouroneacrefarm.com. https://ouroneacrefarm.com/2015/03/15/poultry-predator-identification-a-guide-to-tracks-and-sign/

Livestock and Poultry Predator ID Guide. (n.d.). Benton County, Oregon.

Macer, D. (2019). Ethical Poultry and the Bioethics of Poultry Production. The Journal of Poultry Science, 56(2), 79–83. https://doi.org/10.2141/jpsa.0180074

Malnourished conure. (2012, September 3). Parrot Forum Parrot Owners Community. https://www.parrotforums.com/threads/malnourished-conure.22576/

Matthews, S. (2016, September 16). An Organic Chicken Farm in Georgia Has Become an Endless Buffet for Bald Eagles. Audubon. https://www.audubon.org/magazine/fall-2016/an-organic-chicken-farm-georgia-has-become-endless

Mental Well-being. (n.d.). Org.Nz. https://kids.spcaeducation.org.nz/animal-care/chickens/mental-wellbeing/

Mitchell, A. (n.d). A Simple Guide to the Nutritional Requirements of Poultry. Thepoultrysite.com. https://www.thepoultrysite.com/articles/a-simple-guide-to-the-nutritional-requirements-of-poultry

Nicolaides, C. (1932). Fertility and Hatchability Studies in Poultry. University of Massachusetts Amherst. https://doi.org/10.7275/8V9B-8506

Oloyo, A., & Ojerinde, A. (2020). Poultry Housing and Management. In A. A. Kamboh (Ed.), Poultry - An Advanced Learning. IntechOpen.

O'Connell, N. (2022, May 12). Improved Housing Standards for Commercial Poultry. Queen's University Belfast. https://www.qub.ac.uk/Research/case-studies/improving-housing-standards-commercial-poultry.html

Pecking Order: Understanding Chickens' Social Dynamics. (2022, October 31). Strombergs. https://www.strombergschickens.com/blog/pecking-order-understanding-chickens-social-dynamics/

Pierce, R. (2022, November 18). 15 Ways to Deal with Aggressive Ducks. The Happy Chicken Coop. https://www.thehappychickencoop.com/15-ways-to-deal-with-aggressive-ducks/

Poisbleau, M., Fritz, H., Guillon, N., & Chastel, O. (2005). Linear Social Dominance Hierarchy and Corticosterone Responses in Male Mallards and Pintails. Hormones and Behavior, 47(4), 485–492. https://doi.org/10.1016/j.yhbeh.2005.01.001

Poultry - Diseases and Treatment. (n.d.). Khamarguru.com.
https://khamarguru.com/poultry/en/diseases-treatment.html

Poultry Housing. (n.d.). State.Pa.Us.
http://www.phmc.state.pa.us/portal/communities/agriculture/field-guide/poultry-housing.html

Praharee, T. P. (2023, November 19). Importance of Conservation of Indigenous Breeds of Livestock and Poultry. Pashudhan Prahree.
https://www.pashudhanpraharee.com/importance-of-conservation-of-indigenous-breeds-of-livestock-and-poultry-2/

Predator Management for Small and Backyard Poultry Flocks. (n.d.). Extension.org. https://poultry.extension.org/articles/poultry-management/predator-management-for-small-and-backyard-poultry-flocks/

Predators of Poultry. (n.d.). Osu.edu. https://ohioline.osu.edu/factsheet/vme-22

Pros and Cons of Supplements. (2021, September 2). Food Darzee.
https://fooddarzee.com/blog/pros-and-cons-of-supplements

Rafter W Ranch. (2023, April 2). The Top 4 Benefits of Pasture-raised Chicken. Rafter W Ranch | Colorado Grass Fed Beef, Lamb, Poultry, Produce. https://rafterwranch.net/top-4-benefits-pasture-raised-chicken/

Rhodes, J. (2022, September 11). Using Chickens for Garden Pest Control & Disease in Orchards. Abundant Permaculture.
https://abundantpermaculture.com/using-chickens-for-garden-pest-control/

Roeder, M. (n.d.). 21-Day Guide to Hatching Eggs. Purinamills.com.
https://www.purinamills.com/chicken-feed/education/detail/hatching-eggs-at-home-a-21-day-guide-for-baby-chicks

Selecting the Right Species of Poultry To Get for a Small or Backyard Poultry Flock. (n.d.). Extension.org. https://poultry.extension.org/articles/getting-started-with-small-and-backyard-poultry/selecting-birds-to-get-for-a-small-or-backyard-poultry-flock/

Should You Get a Chicken for Your Home? (n.d.). Green America.
https://greenamerica.org/green-living/many-benefits-backyard-chickens

Small-scale Poultry Production. (n.d.). Fao.org.
https://www.fao.org/3/y5169e/y5169e05.htm

Smith, T. W. (n.d.). Care and Incubation of Hatching Eggs.
Thepoultrysite.com. https://www.thepoultrysite.com/articles/care-and-incubation-of-hatching-eggs

The Best Way to Hatch Chicken Eggs. (2020, September 6). Dine a Chook.
https://www.dineachook.com.au/blog/incubating-chicken-eggs-pros-and-cons/

The Happy Chicken Coop. (2021, March 11). 9 Healthy Treats Your Chickens Will Love. The Happy Chicken Coop.
https://www.thehappychickencoop.com/9-healthy-treats-your-chickens-will-love/

The Hidden Lives of Ducks and Geese. (2010, June 22). PETA. https://www.peta.org/issues/animals-used-for-food/factory-farming/ducks-geese/hidden-lives-ducks-geese/

THL. (2021, January 19). Actory-Farmed Chickens: The Cruelty of Chicken Farms. Thehumaneleague.org. https://thehumaneleague.org/article/factory-farmed-chickens

Turkey Welfare. (n.d.). Org.uk. https://www.ciwf.org.uk/farm-animals/turkeys/turkey-welfare/

Vanmetre, D. (2008). Infectious Diseases of the Gastrointestinal Tract. In Rebhun's Diseases of Dairy Cattle (pp. 200–294). Elsevier.

Virbac. (2019, April 25). How To Choose Good Feed for Your Poultry. Virbac.com. https://in.virbac.com/poultry/health-care/nutrition/how-to-choose-good-feed-for-your-poultry

What Are the Potential Risks Associated With Using Livestock Feed Supplements? (n.d.). SciSpace - Question. https://typeset.io/questions/what-are-the-potential-risks-associated-with-using-livestock-1m48uzjs2m

What is Small Animal Foraging? (1 C.E., January 1). Kaytee.com; Kaytee: Pet Supplies | Kaytee Products. https://www.kaytee.com/learn-care/small-animals/what-is-foraging

Why Nutrition Is So Important for Your Hens.(n.d.). ForFarmers UK.

Wild Turkey identification. (n.d.). Allaboutbirds.org. https://www.allaboutbirds.org/guide/Wild_Turkey/id

Willis, K., & Ludlow, R. T. (2016, March 26).11 Misconceptions About Chickens, Eggs, and So On. Dummies. https://www.dummies.com/article/home-auto-hobbies/hobby-farming/chickens/11-misconceptions-about-chickens-eggs-and-so-on-144654/

Worksheet Freelancer. (2019, March 8). Quail Facts, Worksheets, Habitat, Diet, Characteristics & Breeding for Kids.KidsKonnect. https://kidskonnect.com/animals/quail/